ABOUT DAYS OF H

This book is a day by da... historical events. Each day is linked to an event which could be your birthday or any special occasion in your life so you find yourself learning about events and about yourself as well. This book is part of an on going compilation of contributions to human existence sharing knowledge of developments across all areas of interest. The events have been compiled from a global perspective to suit your interests and investigative research. You are welcome to this unique experience.

Memorable days have several benefits. They serve as a kind of shorthand for important events of history. All day, everyday, everywhere around the world events happen, people build and destroy, people fight and negotiate, each action stands as a distinct event. The dates compiled in this book range from the birthdays of famous and infamous individuals who have contributed to human development and advancement. The events also vary from triumphs to tragedies that had occurred at different times and at different locations around the world.

www.daysofhisory.org

Days of History

This book is a compilation of contributions to human existence sharing knowledge of developments across all areas of interest. The events have been compiled from a global perspective to suit general interests and investigative research.

© Copyright 2013 – JOS Foundation
All Rights Reserved.

ISBN 978-0-9927203-0-8

Published by
Joseph Olawole Shojobi Foundation
www.daysofhistory.org

With the Compliments of:
Dr. Joseph Olawole Shojobi
Found:

Acknowledgement

Appreciation to all members of the Joseph Olawole Shojobi Foundation for their moral and financial support in the publication of this book which will be used to promote academic excellence through scholarships and interactive learning projects.

DAYS OF HISTORY

Jan. 1, 1600
- Scotland begins its numbered year on January 1 instead of March 25.

Jan. 1, 1772
- The first traveler's cheques, which can be used in 90 European cities, go on sale in London.

Jan. 1, 1788
- The Times, London s oldest running newspaper, was first published.

Jan. 1, 1797
- Albany became the capital of New York state, replacing New York City.

Jan 1, 1862
- The US established its 1st income tax.

Jan 1, 1945
- France was admitted to the United Nations.

Jan 1, 1958
- Treaties establishing the European Economic Community went into effect.

Jan 1, 1983
- Pope John Paul II declared this year to be an extraordinary Holy Year to mark the 1,950th anniversary of the death and resurrection of Jesus Christ in year 33.

Jan 1, 1998
- In Russia the government knocked 3 zeroes off the national currency. The old ruble notes will be exchangeable until 2002.

Jan 2, 1777
- American Revolutionary War: American forces under the command of George Washington repulsed a British attack at the Battle of the Assunpink Creek near Trenton, New Jersey.

Jan. 2, 1777
- American Revolutionary War: American forces under the command of George Washington repulsed a British attack at the Battle of the Assunpink Creek near Trenton, New Jersey.

Jan. 2, 1800
- Free black community Philadelphia petition Congress to abolish slavery.

Jan. 2, 1818
- The British Institution of Civil Engineers is founded

Jan. 2, 1860
- The discovery of the planet Vulcan is announced at a meeting of the Academie des Sciences in Paris

Jan. 2, 1919
- Lithuania gains independence

Jan. 3, 1777
- During the American Revolution, Gen. George Washington defeated the British at Princeton and drove them back toward New Brunswick. Washington then established winter quarters at Morristown, New Jersey. During the long harsh winter, Washington's army shrank to about a thousand men as enlistments expired and deserters fled.

Jan. 3, 1848
- Joseph Jenkins Roberts is sworn in as the first president African Republic of Liberia.

Jan. 3, 1986
- The Shogunate was abolished in Japan and Meiji dynasty was restored.

Jan. 3, 1888
- The refracting telescope at the Lick Observatory, measuring 91 cm in diameter, is used for the first time. It was the largest telescope in the world at the time.

DAYS OF HISTORY

Jan. 3, 1888
- The drinking straw was patented by Marvin C. Stone.

Jan. 3, 1924
- British Egyptologist Howard Carter found the sarcophagus of Tutankhamen in the valley of the Kings near Luxor after several years of searching.

Jan. 3, 1946
- An Englishman known during World War II as "Lord Haw Haw" (Williams Joyce) was hanged for treason in London. Joyce had broadcast Nazi propaganda via radio from Germany to Britain during the war.

Jan. 3, 1959
- Alaska was admitted as the 49th U.S. State with a land mass almost one-fifth the size of the entire lower 48 states.

Jan. 4, 1974
- Richard Nixon receives a subpoena which required him to show tapes which would lead to evidence regarding 1972 burglary of the Democratic National Headquarters located in the Watergate complex.

Jan. 4, 1923
- A surprise attack by members of the Ku Klux Klan on a black residential area of Rosewood, Florida left eight people dead.

Jan. 4, 1936
- Billboard Magazine publishes the first pop music chart that is based on national record sales in the USA.

Jan. 4, 1948
- Burma becomes an independent nation no longer under control of the British. Independence to Burma was originally granted by Japan in 1943 after Japan had temporary control over it.

Jan. 4, 1948
- The Arabs and Jews battle for control of the Wailing Wall. This is considered to be one of the holiest shrines in the entire city.

Jan. 4, 1948
- A train collision had occurred in Sangi, Pakistan. The Zakara, a train which typically traveled between Multan and Karachi, took an overnight trip on January 4th was suddenly sent down an alternative track.

Jan. 4, 1754
- Columbia University founded, as Kings College (New York City).

Jan. 4, 1863
- 4 wheeled roller skates patented by James Plimpton on NY.

Jan. 4, 1947
- Samuel Colt sells his first revolver pistol to the United States Government

Jan. 4, 1965
- The New York Stock Exchange opens its first permanent headquarters at 10-12 Broad near Wall Street in New York City.

Jan. 1885
- The first successful appendectomy is performed by William W. Grant on Mary Gartside

Jan. 5, 1859
- First steamboat sails, Red River

Jan. 5, 1892
- First Successful auroral photograph made.

Jan. 5, 1895
- French Captain Alfred Dreyfus, convicted of treason, publicly stripped of his rank; later declared innocent.

Jan. 5, 1896
- German physicist, Wilhem Roentgens, discover x-rays.

Jan. 5, 1905
- Charles perrine announces discovery of Jupiter's 7th satelite, Elara

DAYS OF HISTORY

Jan. 5, 1925
- Nellie Tayloe Ross of Wyoming becomes the first female governor in the United States.

Jan. 5, 1940
- FCC hears first transmission of FM radio with clear, static-free signal

Jan. 5, 1940
- The Federal Communication Commission (FCC) got its very first demonstration of FM radio. The new medium, free of interference was developed by Major E. H. Armstrong

Jan. 5, 1993
- Washington sate executes Westly Allan Dodd by hanging (the last legal hanging in America).

Jan. 5, 1995
- Mass celebration in the streets of Lilongwe, Malawi, following the arrest of former president Hastings Kamuzu.

Jan. 6, 1535
- City of Lima Peru founded by Francisco Pizarro.

Jan. 6, 1898
- First telephone message from a submerged submarine, by Simon Lake.

Jan. 6, 1907
- Maria Montessori opens her first school and daycare center for working class children in Rome.

Jan. 6, 1912
- New Mexico is admitted into the United States as the 47th State.

Jan. 6, 1919
- Former President Theodore Roosevelt died in his estate home in Long Island Oyster Bay, N.Y. He was the youngest president ever to take on the office of President of the U.S.

Jan. 6, 1929
- Mother Teresa arrives in Calcutta to begin her work among India's poorest and sick people.

Jan. 6, 1930 -
First diesel engine automobile trip (in a Packard sedan) completed.

Jan. 6, 1974
- Daylight Saving Time commenced nearly, four months early to help in a bid to save energy during the 1973 energy crisis by reducing the requirements for residential lighting, which consumed about 3.5% of electricity in the US and Canada.

Jan. 6, 1987
- Astronomers at University of California saw first sight of birth of a galaxy.

Jan. 6, 1995
- A chemical fire caused during bomb making testing in the Dona Josefa Apartment complex in Manila, Philippines, led to the discovery of planss for project Bonjinka, a mass-terrorist attack to blow up 11 airliners and their approximately 4,000 passengers.

Jan. 7, 1890
- W B Purvis pattents fountain pen.

Jan. 7, 1904
- The distress signal "CQD" is established only to be replaced two years later by "SOS."

Jan. 7, 1913
- Williams M Burton patents a process to "crack" petroleum.

Jan. 7, 1952
- President Harry Truman announces that the United States has developed the hydrogen bomb.

DAYS OF HISTORY

Jan. 7, 1954
- Georgetown-IBM experiment: the first public demonstration of a machine translation system, is held in New York at the head office of IBM.

Jan. 8, 1587
Johannes Fabricius, astronomer who discovered sunspots, was born in Denmark.

Jan. 8, 1838
- Alfred Vail demonstrates a telegraph system using dots and dashes (this is the forerunner of Morse code).

Jan. 8, 1867
- African-American men are granted the right to vote in Washington, D.C.

Jan. 8, 1868·
Frank Dyson was born. He proved Einstein right that light is bent by gravity.

Jan. 8, 1889
- First computer patented.

Jan.8,1889
Dr. Herman Hollerith (1860·1929), statistician for the US Census Bureall. received the 1st US patent for a tabulating machine. It resembled Charles Babagge's Analytical Engine, but used electromagnetic relays instead of metal gears.

Jan. 8, 1912
- The African National Congress is founded.

Jan. 8, 1926
- Abdul-Aziz ibn Saud becomes the King of Hejaz and renames it Saudi Arabia.

Jan. 8, 1935
- A C Hardy patented the spectrophotometer.

Jan. 8, 1941
- Robert BadenPowell (83), founder of the Boy Scout movement, died.

Jan. 8, 1959
- Charles de Gaulle takes office as the first president of France's Fifth Republic.

Jan. 8, 1975
- Ella Grasso becomes Governor of Connecticut, becoming the first woman to serve as a governor in the United States other than by succeeding her husband.

Jan. 8, 1982
- The American Telephone and Telegraph (AT&T) company was broken up as a result of an antitrust suit.

Jan. 8, 1998 -
Ramzi Yousef was sentenced in New York to life in prison for the 1994 bombing of a Philippines airliner and 240 years for masterminding the 1993 bombing of the World Trade Center.

Jan. 9, 1768
- In London, Philip Astley stages the first modern circus.

Jan. 9, 1951
- Life After Tomorrow, first film to receive an "X" rating, premieres

Jan. 9, 1951
- The United Nations headquarters officially opened in New York City.

Jan. 9, 1960 -
President of Egypt Gamal Abdel Nasser opens construction on the Aswan Dam by detonating ten tons of dynamite to demolish twenty tons of granite on the east bank of the Nile.

DAYS OF HISTORY

Jan. 9, 1960
- With the first blast of dynamite, construction work began on the Aswan High Dam across the Nile River in southern Egypt. One third of the project's billion dollar cost was underwritten by te Soviet Union. The dam created Lake Nasser, one of the world's largest reservoir at nearly 2,000 square miles and irrigated over 100,000 acres of surrounding desert. The dam was opened in January of 1971 by President Nikolai Podgorny of the Soviet Union.

Birthday
- Richard M. Nixon (1913 - 1994) the 37th U.S. President, was born in Yorba Linda, California. He served as Vice President under Dwight D. Eisenhower from 1953-61, then made an unsuccessful run for the presidency, narrowly losing to John F. Kennedy. Nixon ran for governor of California in 1962 and lost. He then told reporters he was leaving politics. However, he re-emerged in 1968 and ran a successful presidential campaign against Hubert Humphrey. He won relection by a landslide in 1972, but resigned two years later amid impeachment proceedings resulting from the Watergate scandal.

Jan. 10, 1776
- Common Sense, a fifty page pamphlet by Thomas Paine, was published. It sold/over 500,000 copies in America and Europe, influencing, among others, the authors of the Declaration of Independence.

Jan. 10, 1861
- In events leading to the U.S. Civil War, Florida became the third state to secede from the Union.

Jan. 10, 1863
- The world's first underground railway service opened in London, the Metropolitan line between Paddington and Farringdon.

Jan. 10, 1870
- John D. Rockefeller (1839-1937) and his brother William incorporated the Standard Oil Company of Ohio.

Jan. 10, 1878
- An Amendment granting women the right to vote was introduced in Congress by Senator A.A. Sargent of California. The amendment didn't pass until 1920, forty two years later.

Jan. 10, 1903
- Argentina banned the importation of American beef, because of sanitation problems.

Jan. 10, 1912
- The flying boat airplane, invented by Glenn Curtis, made its first flight" at Hammond sport, New York.

Jan. 10, 1920
- The League of Nations was established as the Treaty of Versailles went into effect.

Jan.10, 1946
- The first General Assembly of the United Nations opens in London. Fifty-one nation are represented .

Jan.10, 1989
- Cuba began withdrawing its troops from Angola, more than 13 years after its first contingents arrived.

Jan. 11, 1787
- William Herschel discovers Titania and Oberon, two moons of Uranus.

Jan. 11, 1879
- Zulu war against British Colonial rule in South Africa begins.

Jan. 11, 1913 -
- The first sedan-type car was unveiled at the National Automobile Show in New York City. The car was manufactured by the Hudson Motor Company.

DAYS OF HISTORY

Jan. 11, 1922
- Insulin first used to treat diabetes (Leonard Thompson, 14, of Canada).

Jan. 11, 1943
- U.S. and Britain relinquish extraterritorial rights in China.

Jan. 11, 1972
- East Pakistan renames itself Bangladesh.

Jan. 11, 1973
- The first graduates from the Open University (OU) were awarded their degrees after two years studying from home.

Jan. 11, 1998
- Islamic extremists attack the villages of Sidi-Hamed and Haouche Sahraoui, in Algeria massacre up to 400 of the local villagers.

Jan. 11, 2003
- In Chicago, Illinois, Governor George Ryan released four prisoners who were on death row.

Jan. 11, 1964
- U.S. Surgeon General, Luther Leonidas Terry, reported that smoking may lead to major health problems including lung cancer.

Jan. 11, 1962
- A major avalanche of rocks and ice from the extinct volcano of Huascaran, Peru's highest mountain in the Andes range buried the village of Ranrahirca and eight other local villages with the loss of over 4000 estimated.

Jan. 11, 2008
- As the fallout continues from the sub-prime mess and pending foreclosures in Countrywide customers, Bank of America announced it would buy Countrywide Financial for $4.1 billion in stock making Bank of America Corp.

Jan. 12, 1755
- Tsarina Elisabeth establishes first Russian University

Jan. 12, 1866
- The Royal Aeronautical Society is formed in London.

Jan. 12, 1879
- Jan 12, British-Zulu War begins as British troops under Lieutenant General Frederic Augustus invade Zululand from the southern African republic of Natal.

Jan 12, 1906
- Football rules committee legalizes forward pass

Jan 12, 1911
- The University of the Philippines College of Law is formally established; three future Philippine presidents are among the first enrollees.

Jan. 12, 1928
- Ruth Snyder (b. 1895) became the first woman to die in the electric chair. She was electrocuted by "state electrician" Robert G. Elliott at Sing Sing Prison in Oddining, New York.

Jan. 12, 1932
- Hattie W. Caraway becomes the first woman elected to the United State Senate.

Jan 12, 1967
- Dr. James Bedford becomes the first person to be cryonically preserved with intent of future resuscitation. Liner, RMS Queen Mary 2, makes its maiden voyage.

Jan. 12, 1970
- Biafra capitulates, ending the Nigerian civil war.

Jan. 12, 1991
- Gulf War: An act of the U.S. Congress authorises the use of military force to drive Iraq out of Kuwait.

DAYS OF HISTORY

Jan 13, 1559
- Elizabeth I crowned of England in Westminister Abbey

Jan 13, 1785
- John Walter publishes the first issue of the Universal Register(later renamed The Times).

Jan 13, 1854
- Anthony Foss patents accordion

Jan. 13, 1893
- The British Independent Labour Party was founded by Reverened Euba.

Jan 13, 1910
- The first public broadcast takes place; a live performance of the opera Cavalleria rusticana is sent out over the airwaves the Metropolitan Opera House in New York City.

Jan. 13, 1913
- Eko Boys High School, Lagos, Lagos Island, Nigeria, was founded by Reverened Euba.

Jan. 13, 1942
Henry Ford patented a method of constructing plastic auto bodies.

Jan. 13, 1972
- Prime Minister Kofi Busia and President Edward Akufo-Addo of Ghana were ousted in a bloodies military coup by Col. Ignatius Kutu Acheamphong.

Jan. 13, 1989
- Douglas Wilder of Virginia became the first African-American governor in the U.S. as he took the oath of office in Richmond.

Jan. 13, 1991
- 42 killed in exhibition soccer match in Johannesburg, South Africa.

Jan. 13, 1992
- Japan apologises for forcing Korean women into sexual slavery (Comfort women) during World War II.

Jan. 14,1539
- Spain annexes Cuba.

Jan. 14, 1639
- The "Fundamental Orders", the first written constitution that created a government, is adopted in Connecticut.

Jan. 14, 1794
- Dr. Jessee Bennet of Edom Va, performs first successful Cesarean section operation on his wife

Jan. 14, 1873
- 'Celluloid' was registered as a, trademark. It was. The wonderful invention of John Hyatt in 1869. While waiting for a patient, he used the celluloid to wrap his Christmas presents.

January 14, 1878
- U.S.Supreme Court rules race separation on trains unconstitutional.

Jan. 14, 1907
- An earthquake in Kingston, Jamaica, kills more than 1,000.

Jan.14, 1949
- Black/Indian race rebellion in Durban, South Africa; 142 die.

Jan 14, 1953
- Yugoslavia elects its first president (Marshal Tito)

Jan.14, 1960
- The parliament passed a motion for Nigeria's Independence.

DAYS OF HISTORY

Jan 14, 1972
- Comedian Redd Foxx, whose last name was really Sanford, debuted on NBC-TV in "Sanford & Son". Demond Wilson starred as Fred Sanford's son.

Jan. 14, 1974
- World Football League founded.

Jan. 15, 1535
- Henry VIII became Supreme Head of the Church in England as a result of the Act of Supremacy following his break with Rome.

Jan. 15, 1759
- British Museum opens in Montague House, London

Jan. 15, 1780
- Continental Congress establishes court of appeals

Jan. 15, 1861
- Steam elevator patented by Elisha Otis.

Jan. 15, 1877
- Lewis M. Terman, psychologist (developed Stanford-Binet IQ test), was born in Indiana.

Jan. 15, 1889
- The Coca-Cola Company, then known as the Pemberton Medicine Company, is originally incorporated in Atlanta, Georgia.

Jan. 15, 1892
- James Naismith publishes the rules of basketball.

Jan. 15, 1936
- The first building to be competed covered in glass is in Toledo, Ohio.

Jan. 15, 1936
- Non-profit Ford Foundation incorporates

Jan. 15, 1943
- The world's largest office building, The Pentagon, is dedicated in Arlington, Virginia.

Jan. 15, 1944
- European Advisory Commission decides to divide Germany.

Jan. 15, 1955 - USSR ends state of war with German Federal Republic

Jan. 15, 1966
- Major Chukwuma Kaduna Nzeogwu leads, junior officers in a S.L. Akintola and Sir Ahmadu Bello were killed. The Prime Minister, and his Finance Minister Chief Festus Okofie Eboh, were abducted and killed.

Jan. 15, 1970
- After a 32-month fight for independence from Nigeria, Biafra surrenders.

Jan. 15, 1970
- Muammar alqaddafi is proclaimed premier of Libya.

Jan. 15, 1976 - Sara Jane Moore sentenced to life for attempting to shoot President Ford.

Jan. 15, 1992
- The Yugoslav federation, founded in 1918, effectively collapsed as the European Community recognised the republics of Croatia and Slovenia.

Jan. 15, 2001
- Wikipedia, a free Wiki content encyclopedia, goes online.

Jan. 16, 1547
- Ivan the Terrible had himself officially crowned the first Russian Czar (Caesar) although he had already ruled Russia

DAYS OF HISTORY

since 1533. His reign lasted until 1584 and brought much needed reforms including new legal code and cultural development. However, during his reign he instituted a campaign of terror against the Russian nobility and had over 3,000 persons put to death. He also killed his son during a fit of rage.

Jan.16, 1786
- The Commonwealth of Virginia enacted the Statute for Religious Freedom authored, by Thomas Jefferson.

Jan 16, 1868
- Refrigerator car patented! by William Davis, a fish dealer in Detroit

Jan 16, 1877
- Color organ (for light shows) patented, by Bainbridge Bishop,

Jan 16, 1883
- The United States Civil Service Commission was established as the! Pendleton Act went into effect.

Jan. 16, 1979
-The Shah of Iran departed his country amid mass demonstrations and the revolt of Islamic fundamentalists led by Ayatollah Ruhollah Khomeini. The Shah had ruled Iran since 1941 and had unsuccessfully attempted to westermise its culture.

Jan. 16, 1991 -The war against Iraq began as Allied aircraft conducted a major raid against Iraqi air defences. The raid on Baghdad was broadcast live to a global audience by CNN correspondents as operation Desert Shield became Desert Storm.

Birthday
-French industrialist ,Andre Michelin (1853-1931),was born in Paris. He started the Michelin Tire Company in 1888, pioneering the use of pneumatic tires on autos.

Jan. 17, 1773
- Tbe Resolution, saiUng under Captain James Cook, became the first ship to cross the Antarctic Circle.

Jan 17, 1861
- Flush toilet patented by Mr. Thomas Crapper (Honest!)

Jan 17,1882
-First Dutch female physician Aletta Jacobs opens office

January 17, 1945
- During World War II Warsaw, Poland, was liberated by Soviet troops.

Jan 17, 1946
- The UN Security Council holds its first session.

Jan 17, 1961
- Former Congolese Prime Minister Patrice Lumumba is murdered in circumstances suggesting the support and complicity of the governments of Belgium and the United States.

Jan. 17, 1966
A Hyrogen bomb accident a d over Palomares, Spain, as an American 8-52 jet collided with its refueling plane. Eight crewmen were killed and the bomber released its H-bomb into the Atlantic.

Birthday
- Benjamin Franklin (1706-1790) was born in Boston, Massachusetts. Considered the Elder Statesman of the American Revolution; he displayed talents as a printer, (author, publisher, philosopher, scientist, diplomat and philanthropist. He signed both the Declaration of Independence and the U.S. Constitution.

DAYS OF HISTORY

Jan 17, 1983
- The tallest department store in the world, Hudson's, flagship store in downtown Detroit closes due to high cost of operating.

Jan 18, 1788
- English settlers arrive in Australia's Botany Bay to setup penal colony

Jan 18, 1884
- Dr. William Price attempts to cremate the body of his infant son, Jesus Christ Price, setting a legal precedent for cremation in the United Kingdom.

Jan 18, 1896
- The X-ray machine is exhibited for the first time.

Jan 18, 1919
- WW I Peace Congress opens in Versailles, France.

Jan. 18, 1991
- Iraq attacks Tel Aviv, and Haifa with Scud missiles, hoping to bring Israel into the Gulf War and turn it into a wider conflict including other Arab nations.

Jan. 18, 1912
- British explorer Robert Falcon Scott arrives at the South Pole only to find that Roald Amundsen, the Norwegian explorer, had preceded them by just over a month.

Jan. 18, 1920
- The Polish flag was blessed on this day. The person who had officiated this Polish flag blessing was Reverend Augustus Krauso.

Jan 18, 1964
- It was announced in a paper dated on this day that four men were lost after a helicopter went down in Vietnam near the Mouth of the Mekong River.

Jan. 18, 1969
- A tragic series of landslides and floods kills nearly 100 people. These caused by an extraordinary amount of rainfall.

Jan. 18, 1977
- A crowded commuter train in a Sydney suburb derailed into a 100-ton bridge causing the bridge to colapse onto the train passengers.

Jan. 18, 1978
- James Cook is the first known European to discover the Hawaiian Islands, which he names the "Sandwich Islands".

Jan 19, 1883
- The first electric lighting system employing overhead wires, built by Thomas Edison, begins service at Roselle, New Jersey.

Jan 19, 1903
- New bicycle race "Tour de France" announced

Jan 19, 1915
- Georges Claude patents the neon discharge tube for use in advertising.

Jan. 19, 1920
- A group of 600 volunteer nurses were on task to help fight against the flu epidemic. It was reported that about 1,200 cases of this sickness had affected people within 24 hour period of this date in Chicago.

Jan. 19, 1929
- A toad known by the name of "Old" Rip that lived in a Texas building for 31 years died on this day. This toad had lived quite a long time without food or water. Furthermore, it is said that Old Rip was put in the cornerstone of the England County courthouse.

DAYS OF HISTORY

Jan. 19, 1957
- Sir Robert Stapledon, the new Governor of Eastern Nigeria, issued a proclamation dissolving the Eastern Region House of Assembly. and ordering general election for March 15.

Jan. 19, 1983
- Apple announces "The Apple Lisa" the first commercial' personal computer to have a graphical user interface GUI and a computer mouse.

Jan 19, 1955
- "Scrabble" debuts on board game market

Jan 19, 1966
- Indira Gandhi elected India's 3rd prime minister.

Jan. 20, 1937
- Franklin D. Roosevelt became the first U.S. President sworn into office in January. It was Second of four inaugurations; the first had. been held four years earlier on March 4, 1933

Jan. 20, 1965
- Alan Freed, the Father of Rock 'n 'Roll in Palm Springs, California. Freed was one of the first radio disc jockeys to programme black music, or race music, as it was termed, for white audiences.

Jan. 20, 1974
- Golfing great Johnny Miller won the Tucson Open Golf Tournament and became the first radio disc jockeys to programme black music, or race music, as it was termed, for white audiences.

Jan. 20, 1978
- Fred Silverrnan quit as head doncho of programming for ABC-IV. He accepted an offer to be president of NBC.

Jan. 20, 1998
- The headline read. "Cloned Calves Offer Promise of Medicines." The calves were cloned from the cells of cow fetuses by University of Massachusetts scientists. James Robl and Steven Stice, who also worked for Advanced Cell Technology Inc.

Jan. 21, 1789
- "The Power of Sympathy", by William Hill Brown, was published (anonymously) in Boston, MA. The book has been called the first American novel.

Jan. 21, 1815
- Horace Wells, dentist, was born. He pioneered the use of medical anesthesia and was the 1 st to use nitrous oxide as a pain killer.

Jan. 21, 1824
- Ashantee defeat the British in Accra, West Africa.

Jan. 21, 1893
- The Tati Concessions Land, former part of Matabeleland, is formally annexed to the Bechuanaland Protectorate, which is'now Botswana.

Jan. 21, 1899
- Opel manufactures its first automobile.

Jan. 21 1901
- Emirs of Kontagora and Bida are defeated by British forces in the continuing campaign against the Sokoto Caliphate.

Jan. 21, 1921
Barney Clark, the 1 st person to receive a permanent artificial heart, was born.

Jan. 21, 1941
- Dow Chemical produced the first ingot of any metal to be extracted from seawater (magnesium Mg, element 12).

DAYS OF HISTORY

Jan. 21, 1961
- Ahmed Sekou Toure is elected president of the republic of Guinea.

Jan. 21, 1976
Supersonic Concorde, first commercial flights, by Britain and France.

Jan. 22, 1862
- The first govemor of the new colony, Henry Stanhope Freeman, became Governor of Lagos Colony.

Jan. 22, 1957
- The New York City "Mad Bomber," George P. Matesky, is arrested in Waterbury, connecticut and is charged with planting more than 30 bombs.

Jan. 22, 1973
- The Supreme Court of United States delivers its decisiong in Roe v. Wade striking down state laws restricting abortion during the first six months of pregnancy

Jan. 22, 1987
- Pennsylvania politician R. Budd Dwyer shoots and kills himself at a press conference on live national television, leading to debates on boundaries journalism.

Jan. 22, 1990
- Robed. Tappan Morris, Jr. is convicted of releasing the 1988 Internet worm, considered the first computer worm on the Internet. Morris created the worm while he was a graduate student at Cornell University.

Jan. 23, 1849
Elizabeth Blackwell was awarded her MD by the Medical Institute of Geneva, New York, thus becoming America's first woman doctor.

Jan. 23, 1907
- Charles Curtis of Kansas became the first person of American Indian ancestry to serve in the U.S. Senate. He later served as vice president under President Herbert Hoover from 1929-33.

Jan. 23, 1937
- In Moscow, 17 leading Communists went on trial accused of partisipating in a plot led by Leon Trotsky to overthrow Stalin's regime and assassinate its leaders. After a seven day trial, 13 of them were sentenced to death. Trotsky fled to Mexico where he was assassinated in 1940.

Jan. 23, 1943
- In North Africa, British forces under Field Marshal Montgomery captured Tripoli in Libya.

Jan. 23, 1968
- The USS Pueblo was seized by North Sea of Japana amid claims the ship was spying. The ship was confiscated and the crew held in captivity until December, with one fatality.

Birthday
- Russian film director, Sergei Eisenste in (1898-1948), was born in Riga, Latvia. He developed a new way of film making utilising artistic montages (series of arbitrary images) to deliver an emotional impact. Prior to him, most film makers showed scenes in chronological sequence. His classic films include Potemkin, Alexander Nevsky, and Ivan the Terrible.

Jan. 24, 41 AD
- Roman Emperor Caligula was assassinated at the Palatine Games by his own officers after a reign of only four years, noted for his madness and cruelty including arbitrary murder.

DAYS OF HISTORY

Jan. 24, 1848
- The California gold rush began with the accidental discovery of the precious metal near Colomar during construction of a Sutter's sawmill. An announcement by President Polk later in the year caused a national sensation and resulted in a flood of "Forty-niners" seeking wealth.

Jan. 24, 1895
- Hawaii's monarchy ended as Queen Liliuokalani was forced to abdicate. Hawaii was then annexed by the U.S. And remained a territory until statehood was granted in 1959

Jan. 24, 1848
- Gold was first discovered in California, in Sutter's mill. When President Polk announced the news in December, the gold rush began.

Jan. 24, 1908
- Robert Baden-Powell organized the first Boy Scout troop in England.

Jan. 24, 1935
- Canned Beer is sold for the first time, in Virginia (United States).

Jan. 24, 1952
- Vincent Massey was the first Canadian to be appointed governor-general of Canada

Jan. 25, 1533
- King Henry VIII marries his second wife, Anne Boleyn, in defiance of pope Clement who had refused to annul his first marriage. The King later broke all ties with Rome and became Supreme Head of the Church in England.

Jan. 25, 1575
- Luanda, the capital of Angola was founded by the portuguese navigator Paulo Dias de Novais.

Jan. 25, 1579
- Holland, Zeeland, Utrecht, Gelderland, Friesland, Groningen and Overyssel form the (Protestant) Dutch Republic with the signing of the Union of Utrecht to defend their rights against Catholic Spain.

Jan. 25, 1791
- The British Parliament passes the Constitutional Act of 1791 and splits the old province of Quebec into Upper and Lower Canada.

Jan. 25, 1905
- Largest diamond, Cullinan (3106 carets), found in South Africa

Jan. 25, 1919
- The League of Nation is founded.

Jan. 25, 1971
- In Uganda, a military coup led by Idi Amin deposed President Milton Obote. Amin then ruled as president dictator until 1979 when he was ousted by Tanzanian soldiers and Ugandan nationalist. During his reign, Amin expelled all Asians from Uganda, and ordered the execution of more than 300,000 tribal Ugandans.

Jan. 25, 1981
- Jiang Qing, the widow of Mao Zedong, is sentenced to death.

Jan. 25, 1985
- "We are the World" is recorded by Pop stars in Los Angeles

Jan. 25, 1986
- The National Resistance Movement topples the government of Tito Okello in Uganda.

Jan. 26, 1788
- The British First Fleet, led by Arthur Phillip, sails into Port Jackson (Sydney Harbour) to establish Sydney, the first permanent European settlement on the continent. Commemorated as Australia Day.

DAYS OF HISTORY

Jan. 26, 1875
- Electric dental drill is patented by George F Green

Jan. 26, 1905
- The world's largest diamond is found near Pretoria, South Africa

Jan. 26, 1911
- Glenn H. Curtiss flies the first successful American Seaplane.

Jan. 26, 1924
- St. Petersburg is renamed Leningard.

Jan. 26, 1926
- Television first demonstrated (J. L Baird, London).

Jan. 26, 1950
- India becomes a republic, ceasing to be a British dominion.

Jan. 26, 1950
- The Constitution of India comes into force, forming a republic. Rajendra Prasad is sworn in as its first President of India. Observed as Republic Day in India.

Jan. 26, 1991
- Mohamed Siad Barre is removed from power in Somalia, ending centralised government, and is succeeded by Ali Mahdi.

Jan. 26, 1992
- The 160 officers from the ranks of Major in the Nigerian Army, Squadron Leader in the Nigerian Air Force and Commanders in the Nigerian Navy on Course 15 of the Command and Staff College, Jaji, left Kaduna for Lagos on September 23 and their airplane. Hercules C-130, crashed in Ejigbo, Lagos. 163 die.

Jan. 26, 1994
- Romania became the first former Cold War foe to join the North Atlantic Treaty Organization (NATO) following the collapse of the Soviet Union.

Jan. 27, 1736
- Abdication of Stanislas, last king of Poland

Jan. 27, 1785
- The University of Georgia is founded, the first public university in the United States.

Jan. 27, 1880
- *Thomas Edison* patents electric incandescent lamp.

Jan. 27, 1888
- The National Geographic Society *is* founded in Washington, D.C.

Jan 27, 1900
- Social Democrat Party of America (Debs' party) holds first convention.

Jan. 27, 1910
- Thomas Crapper, said to be the inventor and developer of the flush toilet mechanism that most of us use, died on this day,

Jan 27, 1918
- 'Tarzan of the Apes," first Tarzan film, premieres Broadway Theater

Jan. 27, 1944
- Soviet General Govorov announced the lifting of the blockade of Leningrad. During the 900-day Nazi siege, an estimated one million persons inside the city died of disease, starvation and shelling.

DAYS OF HISTORY

Jan. 27, 1945
- The Soviet army liberated Auschwitz death camp near Krakow in Poland, where the Nazis had systematically murdered an estimated 2,000,000 persons, including 1,500,000 Jews.

Jan. 27, 1948
- Wire Recording Corporation of America announced the first magnetic wire recorder. The Wireway' machine with a built-in oscillator sold for $149.50.

Jan. 27, 1967
- Tragedy struck on the launch pad of Apollo 204, scheduled to be the first Apollo manned mission. A flash fire in the command module during a preflight test killed astronauts Virgil Grissom, Edward White and Roger Chaffee. After the disaster, the mission was officially designated Apollo 1.

Jan. 28, 1724
- The Russian Academy of Sciences is founded in St. Petersburg by Peter the Great, and implemented by Senate decree. It is called the St. Petersburg Academy of Sciences until 1917.

Jan. 28, 1820
- A Russian expedition led by Fabian Gottlieb von Bellingshausen and Mikhail Petrovich Lazarev discovers the Antarctic continent approaching the Antarctic coast.

Jan. 28, 1937
- Testing of the Rolls Royce had begun on this day. The first model that appeared on the streets a few years after World War II ended was the Rolls Royce Silver Wraith.

Jan. 28, 1942
- Five power stations are blown up by pro-Axis saboteurs in an attempt to destabilise the Rand gold mines, South Africa.

Jan. 28, 1968
- The new Biafran currency went public and the Nigerian pound was not accepted as an exchange unit.

Jan. 28, 1970
- Cairo suburbs are attacked by Israeli jet fighters.

Jan. 28, 1878
- The first telephone switchboard was installed -in New Haven, Connecticut. The phone company that owned the switchboard had 21 subscribers.

Jan. 28, 1986
- The space shuttle Challenger explodes just after liftoff, killing the seven astronauts aboard, this was the 10th trip for Challenger and included a teacher from New Hampshire, Christ Macauliffe, among the astronauts.

Jan. 28, 1993
- Troops in Zaire run riot, killing the French Ambassador.

Jan. 29, 1886
- Karl Benz patents the first successful gasoline-driven automobile.

Jan. 29, 1896
- Emile Grubbe is first doctor to use radiation treatment for breast cancer.

Jan. 29, 1922
- Union of Costa Rica, Guatemala, Honduras and El Salvador dissolved.

Jan. 29, 1924
- Ice cream cone rolling machine patented by Carl Taylor, Cleveland.

Jan. 29, 1953
- First movie in Cinemascope (The Robe) premieres.

DAYS OF HISTORY

Jan. 29, 1980
- A cabinet office statement said that president Shehu Shagari approved the deportation of Alhaji Shugaba Abdurahman because he was a security risk.

Jan. 29, 1980
- President Shehu Shagari appointed and deployed 16 officers as his special assistants for liaison with the state governments among them was Mr. Jolly Tanko Yusuf for Kaduna state.

Jan. 31, 1747
- The first venereal diseas es clinic opens at London Lock Hospital.

Jan. 31, 1851
- Gail Borden announced the invention of evaporated milk.

Jan. 31, 1876
- The United States orders all Native Americans to move into reservations.

Jan. 31, 1891
- The first attempt at a Portuguese republican revolution breaks out in the northern city of Porto.

Jan. 31, 1915
- World War I: Germany uses poison gas for the 1st time on the Russians at Bolimov.

Jan. 31, 1943
- German troops surrendered at Stalingrad, marking the first big defeat of Hitler's armies. During the Battle of Stalingrad, 160,000 Germans were killed and 90,000 taken prisoner, including the commander, Friedrich von Paulus, the first German field marshal ever to surrender. The captured Germans were forced to march to Siberia, with few ever returning to Germany.

Jan. 31, 1945
- Eddie Slovik, a 24-year-old U.S. Army private, was executed by a firing squad after being sentenced to death for desertion, the first such occurrence in the U.S. Army since the Civil War.

Birthday
- Jackie Robinson (1919-1972) was born in Cairo, Georgia. He was the first African American to play professional baseball, playing for the Brooklyn Dodgers from 1947 to 1956, chosen as the National League's most valuable player in 1949 and elected to the Baseball Hall of Fame in 1962.

Feb. 1, 1788
- Isaac Briggs and William Longstreet patented the steamboat.

Feb. 1, 1790
- In New York City, the Supreme Court of the United States convenes for the first time.

Feb. 1, 1793
- Ralph Hodgson of Lansingburg, New York patented one of the world's greatest inventions: oiled silk.

Feb. 1, 1884
- Edition one of the Oxford English Dictionary is published.

Feb. 1, 1893
- Thomas A. Edison finishes construction of the first motion picture studio, the Black Maria in West Orange, New Jersey.

Feb. 1, 1946
- Trygve Lie of Norway is picked to be the first United Nations Secretary General,

Feb. 1, 1946
A press conference announced the first electronic digital computer, ENIAC, was held at the University of Pennsylvania.

Feb. 1, 1951
- First X-ray moving picture process demonstrated 1951 - 1st telecast of atomic explosion.

DAYS OF HISTORY

Feb 1, 1963
- Nyasaland (now Malawi) becomes self-governing under Hastings Banda

Feb. 1, 1972
- First scientific hand-held calculator, the HP-35, introduced for $395.

Feb 1, 1979
- The Ayatollah Khomeini is welcomed back to Tehran, Iran after nearly 15 years of exile.

Feb. 1, 1982
- Senegal and the Gambia form a loose confederation known as Senegambia.

Feb. 1, 1998
- Rear Admiral Lillian E Fishbume became the first female African American to be promoted to rear admiral

Feb. 2, 1536
- The city of Buenos Aires, Argentina, was founded by Spanish conquistador Pedro de Mendoza.

Feb. 2, 1709
- Scottish sailor Alexander Selkirk, the inspiration for Daniel Defoe's Robinson Crusoe, was rescued after four years alone on an island off the coast of Chile.

Feb. 2, 1863
- Samuel Langhome Clemens decided to use a pseudonym for the first time on this very day. Now he is better remembered by the name, Mark Twain.

Feb. 2, 1971
- Idi Amin became dictator of Uganda.

Feb. 3, 1690
- The first paper money in America is issued in the Mas sachusetts Bay Colony.

Feb. 3, 1848
- Joseph Jenkins Roberts is sworn in as the first president of the independent African Republic of Liberia.

Feb. 3, 1870
- The 15th Amendment to the U.S. Constitution was ratified, guaranteeing the right of citizens to vote, regardless of race, color, or previous condition of servitude.

Feb. 3, 1904
- Brigadier-General Frederick Lugard's West African Frontier Force breach the 50 foot high walls of Great Kano and capture the city, one of the main centres of the Sokoto Caliphate

Feb. 3, 1943
- One of the most extraordinary acts of heroism during World War II occurred in the icy waters oft Greenland after the U.S. Army transport ship Dorchester was hit by a German torpedo and began to sink rapidly. When it became apparent there were not enough life .jackets, four U.S. Army chaplains on board removed theirs, handed them to frightened young soldiers, and chose to go down with the ship.

Feb. 3, 1957 - The Hamilton Watch Company was the first to introduce an electric watch; now a standard in the watch world.

Feb. 3, 1960
- 'The wind of change is blowing through this continent and, whether we like it or not, this growth of national consciousness is a political fact." Harold Macmillan, British Prime Minister, address ing the South African Parliament in Cape Town.

Feb. 3, 1962
- Pope John XXIII excommunicates Fidel Castro.

Feb. 3, 1970
- Marxist government takes over in Congo.

DAYS OF HISTORY

Feb. 3, 1985
- Israeli government confirms resettlement of 10,000 Ethiopian Jews.

Feb. 4, 1783
- England proclaimed the formal end to the hostilities with the United States.

Feb. 4, 1789
- George Washington is unanimously elected as the first President of the United States by the U.S. Electoral College.

Feb. 4, 1794
- The French legislature abolishes slavery throughout all territories of the French Republic.

Feb. 4, 1861
- Delegates from six southern states met at Montgomery, Ala., to form the Confederate States of America.

Feb. 4, 1936
- Radium becomes the first radioactive element to be made synthetically.

Feb. 4, 1938
- Adolf Hitler takes command of the German Army.

Feb. 4, 1985
- Twenty countries in the United Nations signed a document entitled "Convention Against Torture and Other Cruel, Inhuman or Degrading Treatment or Punishment."

Feb. 5, 1597
- A group of early Japanese Christians are killed by the new government of Japan for being seen as a threat to Japanese society.

Feb. 5, 1917
- The current constitution of Mexico is adopted, establishing a federal republic with powers separated into independent executive, legislative, and judicial branches.

Feb. 5, 1918
- Separation of church and state begins, U.S.S.R

Feb. 5, 1922
- Reader's Digest magazine first published.

Feb. 5, 1924
- The Royal Greenwich Observatory begins broadcasting the hourly time signals known as the Greenwich Time Signal or the "BBC pips."

Feb. 5, 1931
-Maxine Dunlap became the first woman licensed as a glider pilot. She was only airborne for one minute

Feb. 5, 1952
- New York adopts three colored traffic lights.

Feb. 5, 1958
-Game! Abdel Nasser nominated first President of United Arab Republic.

Feb. 5, 1958
Gamel Abdel Nasser is nominated to be the first president of the United Arab Republic.

Feb. 5, 1961
The Soviets launch Sputnik V, the heaviest satellite to date at 7.1 tons.

Feb. 5, 1962
Sun, Moon, Mercury, Venus, Mars, Jupiter and Saturn aligned within a 16 degree arc.

Feb. 5, 1997
- Under international pressure, three of Switzerland biggest banks created a fund worth 100 million Swiss francs for holocaust victims and their families.

DAYS OF HISTORY

February 5, 1989
- Kareem Abdul-Jabar becomes 1st NBA player to score 38,000 points

Feb. 6, 1649
- The claimant King Charles 11 of England and Scotland is declared King of Great Britain, by the Parliament of Scotland. This move was not followed by the Parliament of England ' nor the Parliament of Ireland.

Feb. 6, 1804
- Joseph Priestley, British chemist, died. His work on the isolation of gases led him to discover oxygen in 1774,

Feb. 6, 1911
- Ronald Reagan, Former actor and US (40th) President was born..

Feb. 6, 1933
- The 20th Amendment to the U.S. Constitution was adopted. It set the date for the Presidential Inauguration as January 20, instead of the old date of March 4. It also sets January 3 as the official opening date of Congress.

Feb. 6, 1952
- King George VI of England died. Upon his death, his daughter, Princess Elizabeth, became Queen Elizabeth II, Queen of the United Kingdom of Great Britain and Northern Ireland. Her actual coronation took place on June 2, 1953.

Birthdays
- Aaron Burr (1756-1836) was born in Newark, New Jersey. In 1804, Vice President Burr challenged Alexander Hamilton to a duel over Hamilton's negative remarks and mortally wounded him. Bun" was later tried for treason over allegations he was planning to invade Mexico as part of a scheme to establish his own empire in the Southwest, but was acquitted.

- Ronald Reagan, the 40th U.S. President, was born in Tampico, Illinois, February 6, 1911. Reagan spent 30 years as an entertainer in radio, film, and television before becoming Governor of California in 1966. Elected to the White House in 1980, he survived an assassination attempt and became the most popular President since Franklin Roosevelt.

Feb. 7, 1795
- The 11th Amendment to the U.S. Constitution was ratified, limiting the powers of the Federal Judiciary over the states by prohibiting Federal lawsuits against individual states.

Birthday
- Thomas More (1478-1535) was born in London, England. He was a lawyer, scholar, and held the title Lord Chancellor of England. As a loyal Catholic, he refused to acknowledge the divorce of King Henry VIII from Queen Catherine, and thus the King's religious supremacy. He was charged with treason, found guilty and beheaded in 1535, with his head then displayed from Tower Bridge. 400 years later, in 1935, he was canonized by Pope Pius XI.

Birthday
- English novelist Charles Dickens (1812-1870) was born in Portsmouth, England. He examined social inequalities through his works including; David Copperfield, Oliver Twist, and Nicholas Nickleby. In 1843, he created A Christmas Carol in just a few weeks, an enormously popular work even today.

Feb. 7, 1856
- The colonial Tasmanian Parliament passes the second piece of legislation (the Electoral Act of 1856) anywhere in the world providing for elections by way of a secret ballot.

DAYS OF HISTORY

Feb. 7, 1900
- Labour Party forms in England

Feb. 7, 1935
- The classic board game Monopoly is invented.

Feb 7, 1971
- Women in Switzerland were finally granted suffrage.

Feb. 7, 1992
- The Maastricht Treaty is signed, leading to the creation of the European Union.

Feb. 8, 1587
- Mary Stuart, Queen of Scots, was beheaded at Fotheringhay, England, after 19 years as a prisoner of Queen Elizabeth I. She became entangled in the complex political events surrounding the Protestant Reformation in England and was charged with complicity in a plot to assassinate Elizabeth.

Feb. 8, 1837
- Richard Johnson becomes the first Vice President of the United States chosen by the United States Senate.

Feb. 8, 1865
- Martin Robinson Delany became the 1st black major in US army.

Feb.8, 1879
- Sandford Fleming first proposes adoption of Universal Standard Time at a meeting of the Royal Canadian Institute

February 8, 1900
- British troops are defeated by Boers at Ladysmith, South Africa.

Feb. 8, 1920
- Swiss men vote against women's suffrage.

Feb. 8, 1928
- Scottish inventor J.Blaird demonstrates color-TV.

Feb. 8, 1944
- First black reporter accredited to White House, Harry McAlpin.

February 8, 1958
- Edgar Whitehead succeeds Garfield Todd as premier of South Rhodesia.

Feb. 8, 1964
- Chief Dennis Osadebay, as new premier of Mid-Western Region forms Midwest government comprising 17 man cabinet and 11 parliamentarian. Chief Samuel Jereton Mariere is governor.

Feb. 9, 1825
- The House of Representatives elected John Ouincy Adams president after no candidate received a majority of electoral votes.

Feb. 9, 1863
- Fire extinguisher patented by Alanson Crane

Feb. 9, 1895
- William G. Morgan creates a game called Mintonette, which soon comes to be referred to as volleyball.

Feb. 9, 1900
- The Davis Cup competition is established.

Feb. 9, 1963
- The very first Boeing 727 took off. It became the world's most popular way to fly.

Feb. 10, 1763
- Treaty of paris signed, end the france and Indian war. France ceded Canada and all its North American territories east of the Mississippi to Great Britain.

DAYS OF HISTORY

Feb. 10, 1855
-U.S. citizenship laws amended all children of U.S.citizenship.

Feb. 10, 1863
- The fine extinguisher was patented by Alanson Crane.It became a flaming success...

Feb. 10, 1917
- Johanna Westerdijk installed as the Netherlands first female professor.

Feb. 10, 1923
- Ink paste manufactured for 1st time by Standard Ink Company.

Feb. 10, 1931
- New Delhi becomes capital of India.

Feb. 10, 1933
-The New York City based Postal Telegraph Company introduces the first singing telegram.

Feb. 10, 1940
-Tom and Jerry created by Hanna and Barbera debut by MGM.

Feb. 10, 1961
-Nigeria Fall hydroelectric project begins producing power.

Feb. 10, 1963
-The Federal Prime Minister, Sir Abubakar Tafawa Balewa and the three Regional Pimiers, Sir Ahmadu Bello, Dr. Micheal Okpara and Chief Ladoke Akintola, announced that the result of the national population census held on May 1962 must be done all over again "in view of a loss of confidence in the figures for the various regions.

Feb. 10, 1980
- Robert Gabriel Mugabe narrowly misses a second assassination attempt when a bomb explodes behind his limo.

Feb. 11, 1531
- Henry VIII of England is recognized as supreme head of the Church of England.

Feb. 11, 1752
- Pennsylvannia Hospital, the first hospital in United States, is opened by Benjamin Franklin.

Feb. 11, 1826
-University College London is founded under the name University of London.

Feb. 11, 1929
-Italian dictator Benito Mussolini granted independence to the State of Vatican city and recognized the sovereignty of thepope (Holy See) over the area, measuring about 110 acres.

Feb. 11, 1938
- BBC Television produces the world's first ever science fiction television program, an adaptation of a section of the Karel Capek play R.U.R.which coined the term "robot".

Feb. 11, 1945
-First gas turbine propeller driven airplane flight tested, Downey, California.

Feb. 11, 1951
-Kwame Nkrumah wins parliamentary election in Gold Coast(Ghana).

Feb. 11, 1961
-After a plebiscite, the Northern Cameroun, which before then was administered separately within Nigeria. But Southern Cameroun became part of francophone Cameroun.

Feb. 11, 1978
-Censorship: the People's Republic of China lifts a ban on works by Aristotle, Sharespeare and Dickens.

Feb. 11, 1990
-In South Africa, Nelson Mandela, at age 71, was released from Verster Prison outside Cape Town after serving 27 years of a life sentence on charges of attempting to overthrow the apartheid government.

DAYS OF HISTORY

Feb. 12, 1541
- Santiago, Chile is founded by Pedro de Valdivia.

Feb. 12, 1719
- The Onderlinge van 1719 u.a., the oldest existing life insurance company in the Netherlands is founded.

Feb. 12, 1809
- Abraham Lincoln was born in a log cabin in Kentucky. He served as the 16th US President from 1861 until April 15, 1865, when he was assassinated by actor John Wilkes Booth.

Feb. 12, 1873
- American Congress abolishes bimetallism (value of the monetary unit is defined as equivalent either to a certain quantity of gold or to a certain quantity of silver) aid authorises $1 and $3 gold coins.

Feb. 12, 1877
The first public demonstration of the telephone, Alexander Graham Bell's new invention, was publicly done with a hookup between Boston and Salem, Massachusetts.

Feb. 12, 1909
- America's oldest civil rights organisation, the National Association for the Advancement of Coloured People, was jounded.

Feb. 12, 1809 - Abraham Lincoln was born this day in a fog cabin in Kentucky. He served as the 16th U.S. President from 1861 until April 15, 1965, when he was assassinated by actor John Wilkes Booth. (Died 1865)

Feb. 12, 1909
- The National Association for the Advancement of Colored People (NAACP) is founded.

Feb. 12, 1912 - Pu Yi, the last emperor of the Manchu (Ch'ing) dynasty in China, renounced his throne following the establishment of a republic under Sun Yat-sen.

Feb. 12, 1921
- Winston Churchill becomes British, minister of Colonies

Feb. 12, 1974
- Aleksandr Solzhenitsyn, winner of the Nobel Prize in literature in 1970. is exiled from the Soviet Union.

Feb. 12, 1990
- Carmen Lawrence becomes the first female Premier in Australian history when she becomes Premier of Western Australia.

Feb. 12, 2002
- The trial of former President of Federal Republic of Yugoslavia Slobodan Milosevic begins at the United Nations war crimes tribunal in The Hague. He dies four years later before its conclusion.

Feb. 13, 1633
- Italian philosopher, astronomer a n d mathematician, Galileo Galilei, arrived in Rome to face charges of heresy for advocating Copernican theory, which holds that the Earth revolves around the sun. Galileo officially faced the Roman Inquisition in April of that same year and agreed to plead guilty in exchange for a lighter sentence.

Feb. 13, 1635
- Boston Latin School, the first public school America was established in Boston, Mass.

Feb. 13, 1766
- Thomas Robert Malthus, English demographer and political economist, well known for his theories concerning population was born on this day (Died 1834)

DAYS OF HISTORY

Feb. 13, 1795
- First state university in US opens, University of North Carolina

Feb. 13, 1894
- Auguste and Louis Lumiere patent the Cinematographe, a combination movie camera and projector.

Feb. 13, 1945
- The Allies began massive bombing raids on Dresden, Germany, starting a four-day firestorm visible for 200 miles that engulfed the historic old city, killing an estimated 135,000 persons.

Feb. 13, 1960
- France tested its first atomic bomb in the Sahara Desert.

Feb. 13, 1976
- Nigeria Head of State, General Murtala Mohammed, was killed in an abortive coup attempt led by Lt. Col. Buka Suka Dimka. His car was ambushed while en route to his office at Dodan Barracks, Lagos.

Birthday
- American artist, Grant Wood (1892-1942), was born near Anamosa, Iowa. Best known for his painting" American Gothic featuring a farm couple.

Feb. 14
- February 14 is internationally known as Valentine's Day, named after Saint Valentinus of Terni, in. Italy, executed in 270.

Feb. 14, 1817
- Frederick Douglass, African-American abolitionist was bom

Feb. 14, 1819
- Christopher Latham Sholes, inventor of the first practical typewriter, was bom.

Feb. 14, 1849
- Photographer Mathew Brady took the first photograph of a U.S. President in office, James Polk.

Feb. 14, 1849
- The first photograph of a U.S. President was taken by Matthew Brady in New York City.

Feb. 14, 1924
- The International Business Machines Corporation (IBM) Corporation founded by Thomas Watson.

Feb. 14, 1924
- Thomas Watson opens *IBM*

Feb. 14, 1929
- The St. Valentine's Day massacre occurred in Chicago as seven members of the Bugs Moran gang were gunned down by five of Al Capone's) mobsters posing as police.

Feb. 14, 1929
- Members of Al Capone's gang killed rival gang members in the St. Valentine's Day massacre.

Feb. 14, 1957
- Georgia Senate unanimously approves Senator Leon Butts' bill barring blacks from playing baseball with whites.

Feb. 14, 1966
- Australia introduces 1st decimal currency postage stamps.

Feb. 15, 1978
- Leon Spinks beats Muhammad Ali in the 15 the round for heavyweight boxing title.

Feb. 15, 1972
- President Velasco Ibarra of Ecuador deposed for the 4th time.

DAYS OF HISTORY

Feb. 15, 1971
- After 1,200 years Britain abandons 12-shilling system for decimal.

Feb. 15, 1956
- Pirates and Kansas City A's cancel an exhibition game in Birmingham Alabama, because of local ordinance barring black from playing against white.

Feb. 15, 1936
- Hitler announces building of Volkswagen's (starting slug-bug game).

Feb. 15, 1918
- First WWI U.S. Army troop ship torpedoed and sunk by Germany, off Ireland.

Feb. 15, 1879
Congress authorises women lawyers to practise before Supreme Court.

Feb. 15, 1835
- The first constitutional law in modem Serbia was adopted.

Feb. 15, 1852
- Great Ormond St. Hospital for Sick Children, London, admits its first patient.

Feb 15, 1804
- New Jersey becomes last northern state to abolish slavery

Feb 15, 1933
- In Miami, Fiorida, Giuseppe Zangara attempts to' assassinate President-elect Franklin D. Roosevelt, but instead shoots Chicago, Illinois **Mayor** Anton J.Cermak, who **dies** of his wounds on March 6, 1933.

Feb 15, 1971
- Britain changes its currency to the decimal system

Feb 15, 1982
- The world's largest oil rig (The **Ocean Ranger**) **sank** in the storm-tossed north Atlantic with the loss of 84 crew members

Feb. 16, 1918
- The Council of Lithuania unanimously adopts the Act of Independence, declaring Lithuania an independent state.

Feb. 16, 1937
- Wallace H. Carothers receives a United States patent for nylon.

Feb. 16, 1947
- Canadians are granted Canadian citizenship after 80 years of being British subjects. Prime Minister William Lyon Mackenzie King becomes the first Canadian citizen.

Feb 16, 1956
- Britain abolishes death penalty.

Feb. 17, 1600
- Italian philospher, alchemist, and Copernican theory advocate Giordano Bruno was burned at the stake for heresy by the Inquisition.

Feb. 17, 1854
- Britain recognises the independence of Orange Free State (South Africa).

Feb. 17, 1867
- First ship passes through Suez Canal

Feb. 17, 1876
- Sardines first canned by Julius Wolff-Eastport, Maine.

February 17, 1885
- Bismarck gives Carl Peters' firm management of East-Africa.

Feb. 17, 1911
- The First Electric Self Start was installed in a Cadillac by GM. Up till this time all cars needed to be started by cranking a starting handle which was hard work and caused multiple minor injuries when the car backfired during the starting process.

Feb. 17, 1933
- Newsweek magazine is published for the first time

DAYS OF HISTORY

Feb. 17, 1964
- U.S. House of Representatives accept Law on the civil rights

Feb. 17, 1969
- Golda Meir sworn in as Is rael's 1st female prime minister

Feb. 17, 1972
- British Parliament votes to join European Common Market

Feb. 17, 1964
- Gabonese president Leon M'ba is toppled by a coup and his archrival, Jean-Hilaire Aubame, is installed in his place.

Feb. 17, 1965
- Gambia becomes the smallest sovereign state in Africa and the last of Britain's West African colonies to gain independence.

Feb. 17, 2008
- Kosovo declares independence from Serbia.

Feb. 18, 1478
- George, Duke of Clarence, convicted of treason against his older brother, Edward IV of England. He is executed privately at the Tower of G5ndbn.

Feb. 18, 1546
- Martin Luther, German leader of the Protestant Reformation, died.

Feb. 18, 1885
- Mark Twain's Adventures of Huckleberry Finn is published for the first time.

Feb. 18, 1900
- Ajax soccer team forms in Amsterdam

Feb. 18, 1930
- While studying photographs taken in January, Clyde Tom-baugh discovers Pluto.

Feb. 18, 1930
- Pluto, the ninth planet in the solar system, is discovered by American astronomer, Clyde Tombaugh.

Feb. 18, 1962
- France and Algerian Moslems negotiate truce to end seven-year-old war.

Feb 18, 1977
- In Nigeria soldiers from the army of Gen. Obasanjo raided Kalakuta, the com munal home of singer Fela Anikulapo-Kuti.

Feb. 18, 1977
- Soldiers raid Kalakuta, the communal horhe of Fela Anikulapo-Kuti, in Lagos. Fela's mother, Funmilayo (77) is thrown from a second- storey window and later dies from her injuries. The compound is burned and a fire brigade truck is prevented from reaching the site. Fela wrote the song "Coffin for Head of State" to describe how he and his followers carried his mother's coffin to present it to Head of State, Gen. Olusegun Obasanjo.

Feb. 19, 1807
- Vice-President Aaron Burr arrested in Alabama for treason; later found innocent.

Feb. 19, 1831
- First practical U.S. coal-burning locomotive makes first trial run, Pennsylvania

Feb. 19, 1861
- Serfdom is abolished in Russia.

Feb. 19, 1878
- Thomas Alva Edison patents gramophone (phonograph)

Feb. 19, 1919
- Pan-African Con gress, organized by W. E. B. Du Bois (Paris)

DAYS OF HISTORY

Feb. 19, 1920
- Netherlands joins League of Nations

Feb.19,1937
- An assassination attempt on the Italian Viceroy General, Rudolfo Graziani, is made by Ethiopain rebels.

Feb. 19, 1938
- This was a day of extreme tension and anxiety in Berlin, Germany. On this day, Hitler gave a much-anticipated speech, which was delivered to the third Reich (Nazi Germany Government).

Feb. 19, 1942
- President Roosevelt signs Executive Order 9066, a controversial World War II policy with lasting consequences for Japanese Americans.

Feb. 19, 1959
- Britain, Turkey and Greece sign joint agreement giving Cyprus independence.

Feb. 19, 1969
- First Test flight of Boeing 747 jurnbo jet

Feb. 19, 1985
- Canned and bottled Cherry Coke introduced by Coca-Cola

Feb. 19, 1997
- Deng Xiaoping, the last of China's major Communist revolutionaries, died at age 93. He had ruled China from 1978 until he retired in 1990, but his influence remained strong until his death.

Feb. 19, 2008
- Fidel Castro who has ruled Cuba since the revolution in 1959 decides to end his presidency of the country after nearly 50 years.

Feb. 20,1547
- Edward VI of England was crowned King of England at Westminster Abbey.

Feb. 20,1798
- Louis Alexandra Berthier removed Pope Pius VI from office.

Feb. 20, 1873
- The University of California opened its first medical school in San Francisco, California.

Feb. 20,1901
- Ali Mohammed Neguib, Egyptian general and statesman is born in Khartoum.

Feb. 20,1920
- Egyptian Christian Copt Premier, Butros Ghali, is assassinated. Ghali, supported by the British was targeted by Islamic Nationalist fanatics.

Feb. 20,1943
- German Field Marshal, Erwin Rommel, broke through American lines at Kasserine Pass in North Africa as inexperienced U.S. troops lost their first major battle of World War II in Europe, with 1,000 Americans killed.

Feb. 20,1971
- General Idi Amin Dada was appointed President of Uganda.

Feb. 20,1975
- Margaret Thatcher was elected Leader of the British Conservative Party.

Feb. 20, 1975
- The Union of Soviet Socialist Republic conducted a nuclear test at Semipalitinsk, Eastern Kazakhstan, USSR.

Feb. 21,1795
Freedom of worship established in France under constitution.

Feb. 21,1804
- The first ever steam train to run on rails is demonstrated by Richard Trevithick

DAYS OF HISTORY

Feb. 21, 1842
- First known sewing machine patented in U.S., John Greenough, Washington D.C.

Feb. 21, 1848
- Karl Marx and Friedrich Engels publish the Communist Manifesto.

Feb. 21, 1857
- Congress outlaws foreign currency as legal tender in U.S.

Feb. 21, 1858
- Edwin T. Holmes installs first electric burglar alarm(Boston, Massachusetts)

Feb. 21, 1878
- First telephone book issued, 50 subscribers (New Harbor, Connecticut).

Feb. 21, 1922
- Great Britain grants Egypt independence

Feb. 21, 1947
- In New York City Edwin Land demonstrates the first "instant camera", the Polaroid Land Camera, to a meeting of the Optical Society of America.

Feb. 21, 1965
- In New York City, Malcolm X, an .African American nationalist and religious leader, is assassinated by rival Black Muslims while addressing his Organization of Afro-American Unity at the Audubon Ballroom in Washington

Feb. 21, 1970
- Jackson 5 make TV debut on American Bandstand

Feb. 22, 1371
- Robert II succeeded to the throne of Scotland, beginning the Stuart dynasty.

Feb. 22, 1732
- George Washington, the first president of the United States, was born.

Feb. 22, 1819
- By the Adams-Oni's Treaty, Spain sells Florida to the United States for $5m.

Feb. 22, 1907
First cabs with taxi metres begin operating in London.

Feb. 22, 1917
The Russian Revolution begins with a wave of strikes and protests in Petrograd (St.Petersburg).

Feb. 22, 1943
- Sophie School, a 22-year-old activist at Munich University, is executed after being convicted of urging students to rise up and overthrow the Nazi government. School was one of several members of theWhite Rose Society executed.

Feb. 22, 1956
- In Montgomery, Alabama,80 participants in the three-month-old bus boycott voluntarily give themselves up for arrest after an ultimatum from white crty.leaders. Martin Luther King and Rosa Parks were among those arrested. Later in 1956, the US Supreme Court mandated desegregation of the buses.

Feb. 22, 1958
- Egypt and Syria join to form the United Arab Republic.

Feb. 22, 1964
- President Kwame Nkrumah declares a one party state in Ghana.

Feb. 22, 1966
- Premier Apollo Milton Obote, implicated with his army commander General Idi Amin over a scandal of a cache of gold and ivory taken From neighbouring Congo. orders the arrest of five of his cabinet ministers and assumes the presidency.

DAYS OF HISTORY

Feb. 22, 1974
- Organisation of the Islamic Conference summit conference begins in Lahore, Pakistan. Thirty-seven countries are attending. Twenty-two heads of state and government participate.

Feb. 23, 1821
- The Philadelphia College of Apothecaries was established. It was the first pharmacy college in the U.S.

Feb. 23, 1874
- Major Walter Winfield patents a game called "sphairistike" (lawn tennis).

Feb. 23, 1886
- London Times publishes world's first classified advert.

Feb. 23, 1886
- Charles M. Hall completes his invention of aluminum. He produced it using electricity; and just in time for wrapping the 20th century's lunch sandwiches, too!

Feb. 23, 1904
- U.S. acquired control of the Panama Canal Zone for $10 million

Feb. 23, 1905
- Chicago attorney, Paul Harris, and three other businessmen meet for lunch to form the Rotary Club, the world's first service club.

Feb. 23, 1919
- Benito Mussolini forms the Fascist Party in Italy.

Feb. 23, 1941
- Plutonium is first produced and isolated by Dr. Glenn T. Seaborg.

Feb. 23, 1947
- The International Organisation for Standardisation is founded.

Feb. 23, 1954
- The first mass inoculation of children against polio with the Salk vaccine begins in Pittsburgh.

Feb. 23, 1988
- Judge stops trial of security chiefs, Halilu Akilu and Kunle Togunoverthe murder of frontline journalist, Dele Giwa. Chief Gani Fawehinmi tells newsmen outside the court shortly after the ruling that he will fight back "in grand style."

Feb. 24, 1821
- Mexico gains independence from Spain.

Feb. 24, 1920
- A fledgling German political party held its first meeting of importance at Hofbrauhaus in Munich; it became known as the Nazi Party, and its chief spokesman was Adolf Hitler.

Feb. 24, 1924
- Mahatma Gandhi was released from jail.

Feb. 24, 1925
- Thermit explosive first used to break up ice jam, Waddington, New York

Feb. 24, 1943
- Rommel is appointed as commander-in-chief, Army Group Africa, during world war II, North Africa.

Feb. 24, 1945
- Egyptian Premier Ahmed Maher Pasha is killed in parliament after reading a decree.

Feb. 24, 1949
- After 42 days of bitter debate, Egypt and Israel sign an armistice on the island of Rhodes. However, the status of Beersheba in the Negev Desert, were dropped from the final agreement.

DAYS OF HISTORY

Feb. 24, 1964
- Nigerian Census figures were released. North, 29,777, 986; East, 12, 388, 646; West, 10,278,500; Mid-West, 2, 533, 337; Lagos, 675, 352.

Feb. 24, 1966
- A military coup overthrew Ghana's President Kwame Nkrumah. He fled to Guinea.

Feb. 24, 1981
- Buckingham Palace announced the engagement of Britain's Prince Charles to Lady Diana Spencer.

Feb. 24, 1989
- Iran's Ayatollah Ruhollah Khomeini offers a USD $3m bounty for the death of *The Satanic Verses* author, Salman Rushdie.

Feb. 25, 1836
- Samuel Colt patented the first revolving barrel multi-shot firearm.

Feb. 25, 1870
- Hiram Rhodes Revels, a Republican from Mississippi, is sworn into the United States Senate, becoming the first African-American ever to sit in the U.S. Congress.

Feb. 25, 1919
- League of Nations set up by Paris Treaty.

Feb. 25, 1932
- Adolf Hitler obtains German citizenship by naturalisation, which allows him to run in the 1932 election for Reichsprasident.

Feb. 25, 1954
- Abdul Nasser appointed Egyptian premier.

February 25, 1964
Cassius Clay (Muhammad AN) became World Heavyweight Boxing champion for the first time by knocking out Sonny Listen in Miami Beach.

February 25, 1977
- 240 US citizens in Uganda are held hostage by Field Marshal Idi Amin Dada.

Feb. 26, 1848
- Karl Marx and Frederick i Engels publish The "Communist Manifesto" in London.

Feb. 26, 1885
- Congress of Berlin gives Congo to Belgium and Nigeria to England.

Feb. 26, 1907
- Royal Oil and Shell merge to form British Petroleum.

Feb. 26, 1916
- Mutual signs Charlie Chaplin to a film contract- Three years later, the 'old' Charlie Chaplin films are released and are very successful at the box office.

Feb. 26, 1930
- First red and green traffic lights installed in Manhattan, New York City.

Feb. 26, 1935
-RADAR (Radio Detection and Ranging) was first demonstrated by Robert Watson-Watt.

Feb. 26, 1962
US Supreme Court disallows race separation on public transportation.

Feb. 26, 1968
- Thirty-two African nations agree to boycott the Olympics because of the presence of South Africa.

Feb. 27, 1557
The 1st Russian Embassy opened in London.

DAYS OF HISTORY

Feb. 27, 1700
- The Pacific Island of New Britain was discovered. It is the largest of group of islands in the South Pacific, NE of New Guinea.

Feb. 27, 1844
- Dominican Republic rebels, under the leadership of Francisco del Rosario Sanchez and Ramson Mella, launched Surprising and gamed-independence from Haiti (National Day).

Feb. 27, 1872
- Charlotte Ray, first Black woman lawyer, 'graduated from Harvard University.

Feb. 27, 1879
- Constantine Fahlberg discovered saccharin, the artificial sweetener

Feb. 27, 1950 -The 22nd Amendment to the U.S. Constitution was ratified, limiting the president to two terms or a maximum of ten years in office.

Feb. 27, 1980
- Robert Mugabe's ZANU-PF won election in Zimbabwe.

Feb. 27, 1991
-In Desert Storm, the 100 hour ground war ended as Allied troops entered Kuwait just four days after launching their offensive against Iraqi forces.

Feb. 27, 1999
- Nigerians went to vote for president between PDP candidate, Olusegun Obasanjo and the APP/AD candidate, Olu Falae.

Birthday
-American poet, Henry Wadsworth Longfellow (1807-1882), was born in Portland,' Maine. Best known for Paul Revere's Ride, The Song of Hiawatha, and The Wreck of the Hesperus.

Feb. 28, 1784
- John Wesley issues "Deed of Declaration" formally establishing the Methodist Church.

Feb. 28, 1844
- During a demonstration of naval fire power, one of the guns aboard the USS Princeton exploded, killing several top U.S. government officials on the steamer ship, and narrowly missed killing President John Tyler.

Feb. 28, 1854
- The Republican Party is founded, in Ripon, Wisconsin, United States

Feb. 28, 1935
DuPont scientist Wallace Carothers invents Nylon.

Feb. 28, 1977
First killer whale born in captivity (Marineland, Los Angeles California)

Feb. 28, 1986
- Swedish Prime Minster Olof Palme (1927-1986) was assassinated in Stockholm exiting a movie theater with his wife.

Feb. 28, 1759
- Pope Clement XIII grants permission for the Bible to be translated into the languages of the Roman Catholic states

Feb. 28, 1784
- John Wesley issues "Deed of Declaration" formally establishing the Methodist Church.

Feb 28, 1922
Egypt is declared a sovereign state by Britain.

DAYS OF HISTORY

Feb. 28, 1954
The first-ever color television sets using the NTSC standard are offered for sale to the general public.

March 1, 1780
- Pennsylvania becomes the first U.S. state to abolish slavery (for new-bom only). It is followed by Connecticut and Rhode Island in 1784, New York in 1785, and New Jersey in 1786. Massachusetts abolished slavery through a judicial decision in 1783.

March 1, 1864
- Rebecca Lee (1831-1895) becomes the first black woman to receive an American medical degree, from the New England Female Medical College in Boston.

March 1, 1872
-Yellowstone National Park is established as the world's first national park.

March 1, 1896
- Henri Becquerel discovers radioactivity.

March 1, 1912
- Captain Albert Berry of the Jefferson Barracks in St. Louis, MO made the first parachute jump from a moving airplane. He jumped from an altitude of 1,500 feet at a speed of 50 mpn.

March 1, 1947
-International Monetary Fund begins operation.

March 1, 1949
- Joe Louis retires as heavyweight boxing champion.

March 1, 1953
- Francis Crick (d.2004) and James Watson discover the structure of DNA-

March 2, 1776
- Americans begin shelling British troops in Boston.

March 2, 1807
- The United States Congress bans slave trade effective in January 1, 1808.

March 2, 1898
- Australia complete a 4-1 series annihilation of England.

March 2, 1944
- A train stops in a tunnel near Salerno in the Apennine Mountains, and more than 500 people on board suffocate and die due to toxic carbon monoxide fumes.

March 2, 1955
- King Norodom Sihanukh of Cambodia's succeeded by his father.

March 2, 1956
- Morocco tears up the Treaty of Fez, declares independence from France.

March 2, 1969
- The two greatest communist powers of the world open fire against each other. The climax of this "clash" occurred in the eastern portion of the U.S.S.R., on the Ussur River between Soviet and Chinese Troops.

March 2, 1970
- The Prime Minister o Rhodesia, Ian Smith, hai declared Rhodesia ; republic.

March 4, 1665
- English king Charles II declares war on Netherlands.

March 4, 1801
- Thomas Jefferson is the first president inaugurated in Washington D.C.

DAYS OF HISTORY

March 4, 1809
- Madison become the 1st president inaugurated in American-made clothes

March 4, 1849
- U.S. had no president, Polks, terra ends on a Sunday, Taylor couldn't be inaugurated, Senator David Atchison's (President pro-tempore) term ended March 3rd.

March 4, 1972
- Libya and U.S.S.R. Signs cooperation treaty

March 4, 1980
- Robert Mugabe wins election to become Zimbabwe's first black prime minister.

March 4, 1681
- King Charles II of England granted a huge tract of land in the New Vlforld to William Penn to settle an outstanding debt. The area later became Pennsylvania.

March 5, 1624
- Class-based legislation was passed in the colony of Virginia, exempting the upper class from punishment by whipping.

March 5, 1770
- British troops taunted by a crowd of colonists fired on an unruly mob in Boston and killed five citizens in what came to be known as the Boston Massacre.

March 5, 1836
- Samuel Colt manufactures 1 st pistol, 34-caliber 'Texas" model

March 5, 1868
- The U.S. Senate convened as a court to hear charges against President Andrew Johnson during impeachment proceedings. However, the effort to remove him failed in the Senate by just one vote and he remained in office.

March 5, 1868
- Stapler patented in England by C. H. Gould.

March 5, 1900
- American Hall of Fame found.

March 5, 1912
- The Italians became the first to use dirigibles (An airship) for military purposes, using them for reconnaissance flights behind Turkish lines west of Tripoli.

March 10, 1876
- Alexander Graham Bell makes the first successful telephone call by saying "Mr. Watson, come here, I want to see you."

March 10, 1893
- New Mexico State University cancels its first graduation ceremony; its only graduate Sam Steele was robbed and killed the night before.

March 10, 1959
- Tibetan uprising: Fearing an abduction attempt by China, 300,000 Tibetans surround the Dalai Lama's palace to prevent his removal.

March 10, 1964
- A new party called the Nigerian National Democratic Party (NNDP) was formed in Western Region.

March 10, 1969
- James Earl Ray was sentenced in Memphis, Tennessee, to 99 years in prison for the murder of Martin Luther King, Jr., In April 1968.

March 10, 1982
- President Reagan proclaims economic sanctions against Libya 1987-Vatican formal opposition to test-tube fertilization and embryo transfer.

DAYS OF HISTORY

March 11, 1302
- Romeo & Juliet's wedding day, according to Shakespeare.

March 11, 1906
- The Simplified Spelling Board is announced with Andrew Carnegie funding the organisation, to be headquartered in New York City. In August, President Theodore Roosevelt issued an executive order mandating simplified spelling in all government administrative documents.

March 11, 1911
- The Cadillac Division of General Motors demonstrates the first electric self-starter, enabling women to drive alone. Charles Kettering created the first successful electric self-sterter for Cadillac.

March 11, 1918
- Moscow becomes capital of revolutionary Russia.

March 11, 1918
- First confirmed cases of the Spanish flu are observed at Fort Riley, Kansas.

March 11, 1971
- Federal Communications Commission states that television networks ABC, NBC and CBS must have a limited three-hour nightly programme service now called 'Prime Time' Prime Time? Began in September of 1971.

March 12, 1755
- The 1st steam engine in America was installed to pump water from a mine.

March 12, 1809
- Great Britain signed a treaty with Persia forcing the French out of the country.

March 12, 1894
- Coca-Cola was sold in bottles for the first time.

March 12, 1930
- Indian political and spiritual leader Mohandas K. Gandhi began a 200-mile march to the sea to protest a British tax on salt. The march symbolized his defiance of British Rule over India.

March 12, 1945
- New York became the 1st state to prohibit discrimination by race and creed in employment.

March 12, 1968
- The British-ruled African island of Mauritius became an independent country within the Commonwealth of Nations and many Europeans left the country.

March 12, 1983
- Joshua Mqabuko Nyangol Nkomo has fled Zimbabwe following a failed armed rebellion by Zimbabwe African People's Union (ZAPU) forces in Matabeleland. Robert Mugabe and the Zimbabwe African National Union (ZANU) government reacted strongly.

March 13, 1639
- Cambridge College renamed Harvard University in honour of clergyman, John Harvard

March 13, 1781
- The German-bom English astronomer, Sir William Hersche), discovered the planet Georgium Sidus, later known as Uranus,

March 13, 1933
- Josef Gobbels became German Minister of Information and Propaganda.

March 13, 1943
- A plot to foil Hitler by German army officers failed as a bomb planted aboard his plane failed to explode due to a faulty detonator.

DAYS OF HISTORY

March 13, 1967
- Congo sentenced ex-premier, Moise Tsjombe, to death.

March 13, 1997
- India's Missionaries of Charity chose Sister Nirmala to succeed Mother Teresa as its leader.

Birthday
-Scientist and clergyman, Joseph Priestly (1733-1804), was born in Yorkshire, England. He discovered oxygen and advanced the religious theory of Unitarianism.

March 15, 1391
- A Jew-hating monk in Seville, Spain, stirs up a mob to attack Jews.

March 15, 1493
- Christopher Columbus returns to Spain, concluding his first voyage to the Western Hemisphere.

March 15, 1809
- Joseph Jenkins Roberts, first President of Liberia, is born.

March 15, 1854
- Emil Von Behring, first recipient of the Nobel Prize for medicine in 1901, is born.

March 15, 1892
- New York State unveils the new automatic ballot voting machine.

March 15, 1903
-The British complete the conquest of Nigeria; 500,000 square miles are now controlled by the United Kingdom.

March 15, 1907
- Finland becomes the first European country to give women the right to vote.

March 15, 1913
- President Wilson meets with reporters for what's been described as the first presidential press conference.

Some sources say Wilson's first actual press conference was a week later.

March 16, 1815
- Prince Willem of the House of Orange-Nassau proclaims himself King of the United Kingdom of the Netherlands, the first constitutional monarch in the Netherlands.

March 16, 1827
- The first Afro-American newspaper edited for and by blacks, *Freedom's Journal.* was published in New York.

March 16, 1882
- US Senate ratified a treaty establishing the Red Cross.

March 16, 1935
- Adolf Hitler ordered a German rearmament in violation of the Versailles Treaty. He announced in public Nazi rearmament and the existence of the new German air force, the Luftwaffe.

March 16, 1955
- President Eisenhower upheld the use of atomic weapons in case of war.

March 16, 1958
- The Ford Motor Company produces its 50 millionth automobile, the Thunderbird, averaging almost a million cars a year since the company's founding.

March 16, 1984
- Mozambique and Soutrr Africa signed a pact banning support for one another's internal foes.

March 16, 1999
- Cuban Americans, whose sons were in custody by the INS, began a hunger strike outside the gates of the Krome Detention Center at the edge of the Everglades.

DAYS OF HISTORY

March 17, 624
- Led by Muhammad, the Muslims of Medina defeat the Quraysh of Mecca in the Battle of Badr.

March 17, 1776
- American Revolution: British forces evacuate Boston, Massachusetts after George Washington and Henry Knox place artillery overlooking the city

March 17, 1906
- President Theodore Roosevelt first likened crusading journalists to a man with "the muckrake in his hand" in a speech to the Gridiron Club in Washington, DC, as he criticized what he saw as the excesses of investigative journalism.

March 17, 1959
- The Dalai Lama fled Tibet and went to India, triggering a flood of refugees escaping Chinese rule.

March 17, 1963
- The Western Regional Government announced that it would acquire, "for public purposes" all property in the Region owned by the National Investment and Properties Company in accordance with Coker commission's recommendation and on the Federal Governments White Paper.

March 18, 1229
- German emperor Frederick II crowned himself king of Jerusalem.

March 18, 1532
- English parliament banned payments by English church to Rome.

March 18, 1766,
- Britain repealed the Stamp Act of 1765.

March 18, 1895
- Some 200 blacks left Savannah, Ga., for Liberia.

March 18, 1922
- Mohandas K. Gandhi was sentenced in India to six years' imprisonment for civil disobedience. He was released after serving two years, (see Mar 22) "

March 18, 1938
- Mexican President Lazaro Cardenas nationalized his country's petroleum reserves and took control of foreign-owned oil facilities.

March 18, 1952
- The 1st plastic lens for cataract patients was fitted in Phila.

March 18, 1963
- The US Supreme Court made its Gideon v Wainwright ruling which said poor defendants have a constitutional right to an attorney. Gideon had been forced to defend himself in Florida in Jan 1962, and petitioned the Supreme Court to hear his complaint.

March 19, 1944
- Nazi German soldiers occupied Hungary.

March 19, 1962
- Relative calm returned to Algeria after cease-fire, Ending 7 years of warfare between France and Algeria Nationalists.

March 19, 1963
- In Coast Rica, President John .F.Kennedy and six Latin
American presidents pledged to fight Communism.

March 19, 1965
- Indonesia nationalized all foreign oil companies.

DAYS OF HISTORY

March 19, 1977
- Congolese president Major Marien Ngouabi is assassinated
By a suicide commando during a failed military coup. Ex-
President Alphonse Massemba-Debat is implicated in the Coup
And executed without trial one week later.

March 19, 1978
- The UN Security Council adopted Resolution 425 demanding
That Israel withdraw from Lebanon.

March 19, 1987
- President Reagan, in a news conference, repudiated his policy
Of selling, "I would not go down that road again."

March 21, 1933
- Construction of Dachau, the first Nazi Germany concentration camp, is completed.

March 21, 1935
- Persia officially renamed Iran.

March 21, 1960
- Apartheid: Massacre in Sharpeville, South Africa: Police open fire on a group of unarmed black South African demonstrators, killing 69 and wounding 180.

March 21, 1963
- Alcatraz prison in San Francisco Bay, a harsh maximum security jail which once housed which once house gangster Al-Capone, Close.

March 21, 1962
- Martin Luther King Jr leads 3,200 people on the start of the third and finally successfully civil rights march from Selma to Montgomery, Alabama.

March 21, 1975
- Ethiopia ends monarchy after 3000 years.

March 21, 1980
- US President Jmmy Carter announces a United States boycott of the 1980 Summer Olympics in Moscow to protest the Sviet Invasion of Afghanistan.

March 22, 1765
- Britain enacted the Stamp act to raise money from the American Colonies. This was the first direct British tax on the colonists. The tax covered just about everything produced by the American colonists and began the decade of crisis that led to the American Revolution. The Stamp Act taxed the legal documents of the American colonists and infuriated John Adams.

March 22, 1872
- Illinois became 1st state to require sexual equality in employment.

March 22, 1882
- US Congress outlawed polygamy. The Edmunds-Tucker Act was adopted by the US to suppress polygamy in the territories.

March 22, 1904
- The first color photograph was published in the London Daily Illustrated Mirror.

March 22, 1919
- The first international airline service was inaugurated on a weekly schedule between Paris and Brussels.

March 22, 1953
- 2,500 Tribesmen are arrested in Kenya as part of the continuing crackdown by British authonties against the Mau Mau.

DAYS OF HISTORY

March 22, 1977
- President Carter proposed the abolition of the Electoral College.

March 22, 1977
- Indira Gandhi revoked emergency rule and resigned as PM of India.

March 23, 1775
- American Revolutionary War: Patrick Henry delivers his famous speech - "Give me Liberty, or ojve me Death!" -at St. John's Church in Richmond, Virginia.

March 23, 1840
- Draper took first successful photo of the Moon (daguerreotype).

March 23, 1857
- Elisha Otis installed the first modern passenger elevator in the 5-story Haughwout and Co. building at 488 Broadway in New York City.

March 23, 1889
- The Ahmadiyya Muslim Community is established by Mirza Ghulam Ahmad in Qadian India.

March 23, 1880
- John Stevens of Neenah, Wis., patented the grain crushing mill. This mill allowed flour production to increase by 70 per cent.

March 23, 1903
- The Wright brothers obtained an airplane patent.

March 23, 1919
- Benito Mussolini founded his Fascist political movement in Milan, Italy.

March 23, 1933
- The Reichstag passes the Enabling act of 1933, making Adolf Hitler dictator of Germany.

March 23, 1950
- UN World Meteorological Organisation was Established.

March 24, 1663
- Charles II of England awarded lands kriftwn as Carolina in America'tb *eight* members of the -ncteility wn assisted in his restoration

March 24, 1837
- Canada gives African men the right to vote.

March 24. 1882
- Robert Koch announces the discovery of the bacterium responsible for tuberculosis (mycobacterium tuberculosis).

March 24, 1923
- Greece becomes a republic.

March 24. 1972
- The United Kingdom imposes "Direct Rule over Northern Ireland.

March 24, 1976
- In Argentina, the armed force overthrow the constitutional government of President Isabel Peron and start a 7-year dictatorial period self-styled National Reorganization Process.

March 24, 1987
-French Premier Jacoues Chirac signed a contrac Twitn Walt Disney Productions for the creation of a Disneyland amusement park, the first in Europe.

March 24, 1998
- The UN announced a pullout from Afghanistan after the governor of Kandahar slapped the face of a UN employee.

DAYS OF HISTORY

March 24, 1998
- In South Korea the government fired two-thirds of the senior officials at its spy agency in a move to get the agency out of domestic politics.

March 25, 1968
- US performs nuclear test at Nevada Test Site

March 25, 1655
- Saturn's largest moon, Titan, is discovered by Christian Huygens.

March 25, 1807
- The Slave Trade Act becomes law, abolishing the slave trade in the British Empire.

March 25, 1957
- The European Economic Community is established (West Germany, France, Italy, Belgium, Netherlands, Luxembourg).

March 25, 1965
- Civil rights activists led by Martin Luther King, Jr. successfully complete their 4-day 50-mile march from Selma to the capitol in Montgomery, Alabama.

March 25, 1975
- Faisal of Saudi Arabia is shot and killed by a mentally ill nephew

March 25, 1971
- Bangladesh Liberation War. Beginning of Operation Searchlight of Pakistan Army against East Pakistani civilians.

March 25, 1993
- President FW de Klerk admits that six South Africa built six nuclear bombs and states that they have since been dismantled.

March 26, 1780
- First British Sunday newspaper appears (British Gazette and Sunday Monitor)

March 26, 1872
- Thomas J. Martin patents fire extinguisher

March 26, 1878
- Sabi Game Reserve, world's first official designated game reserve, opens

March 26, 1886
- The First cremation in England took place,

March 26, 1934
- The driving test .is introduced in the United Kingdom.

March 26, 1953
- Dr. Jonas Salk announced a new vaccine to prevent poliomyelitis

March 26, 1971
- East Pakistan proclaimed its independence taking the name Bangladesh

March 26, 1979
- The Camp David Accord ended 30 years of warfare between Israel and Egypt Prime Minster Menachem Begnvef Israel and Egyptian President Anwar Sadat signed the treaty of mutual recognition and peace, fostered by U.S. President Jimmy Carter.

March 26, 1989
- First free elections in U.S.S.R.; 190 M votes cast; Boris Yeltsin wins.

March 27, 1836
- Texas Revolution began with the Goliad massacre. Antonio Lopez de Santa Anna ordered the Mexican army to kill about 400 Texans at Goliad, Texas.

March 27, 1871
- The first international rugby football match, England vs Scotland, was played in Edinburgh at Raeburn Place.

DAYS OF HISTORY

March 27, 1970
- Concorde made its first supersonic flight.

March 27, 1977
- The worst accident in the history of civil aviation occurred as two Boeing 747 jets, a. Pan American and KLM, collided on the runway in Santa Cruz de Tenerife, Canary Islands, resulting in 570 deaths. .

March 27, 1995
- Winnie Madikizela-Mandela, the estranged wife of Nelson Mandela, was dismissed from the South African government.

March 27, 1998
- The Food and Drug Administration approved Viagra for use as a treatment for male impotence, the first pill to be approved for this condition in the United States of America.

March 28, 1797
- Nathaniel Briggs OT- New Hampshire patented a washing machine. March 28, 1885 - The Salvation Army was officially organized in the U.S.

March 28, 1891
- The first world-championship for amateur weight lifters was held in London. March 28, 1910 - Henri Fabre becomes the first person to fly a seaplane, the Fabre Hydravion, after taking off from a water runway near Martigues, France.

March 28, 1917
The Women's Army Auxiliary Corps (WAAC) was founded, these were Great Britain's first official service women. March 28, 1922 - The 1st microfilm device was introduced.

March 28, 1930
The cities of Constantinople and Angora changed names to Istanbul and Ankara, Turkey.

March 28, 1933
- German Reichstag conferred dictatorial powers on Hitler.

March 29, 1638
- The first permanent white settlement was established in Delaware. Swedish Lutherans who came to Delaware were the' first to build log cabins in America.

March 29, 1798
- Republic of Switzerland formed.

March 29, 1799
- New York passes a law aimed at gradually abolishing slavery in the state.

March 29, 1848
- Niagara Falls slowed to a trickle for about 30 hours due to an ice jam from Lake Erie in the Niagara River.

March 29, 1886
- Coca-Cola was advertised for the 'first time in the Atlanta Daily. Its -inventor, Dr. John Pemberton, claimed it could cure anything from hysteria to the common cold.

March 29, 1961
- In South Africa Nelson Mandela was- acquitted on a treason charge after a 4 year trial.

March 29, 1967
The first nationwide strike in the 30-year history of the American Federation of Television occurred and lasted for 13, days.

March 29, 1995
- The House of Representatives rejected, 227-204, a constitutional amendment placing term limits on lawmakers, the rejected proposal would have limited terms to 1 2 years in the House and Senate.

DAYS OF HISTORY

March 30, 1855
- First election in Territorial Kansas. Some 5,000 "Border Ruffians" invaded the territory from western Missouri and forced the election of a pro-slavery legislature.

March 30, 1867
- US Secretary of State William H. Seward reached agreement with Russia's Baron Stoeckl to purchase the territory of Alaska for $7.2 million, two cents an acre, a deal roundly ridiculed as "Seward's Folly," "Seward's icebox," and President Andrew Johnson's "polar bear garden." The treaty was signed the nestdy.

March 30, 1870
- The 15th Amendment to the US Constitution, guaranteeing the right to vote regardless of race, was declared in effect by Secretary of State Hamilton Fish.

March 30, 1912
- France is granted the right to create a protectorate over Morocco by its Sultan as part of a treaty agreement signed today in Fez. A French resident-general will be appointed and France will take control of Morocco's international finances.

March 30, 1979
- Anthrax spores leaked from a secret germ-warfare plant and spread over Sverdlovsk (Yekaterinburg), Russia. Over the course of 2 months Tat least 105 people died of anthrax poisoning. Reports did not emerge until October.

March 31, 1492
- Ferdinand and Queen Isabella of Spain issue the Alhambra decree, ordering her 150,000 Jewish subjects to convert to Christianity or face expulsion.

March 31, 1903
- New Zealand aviator Richard Pearse flew a self-made, bamboo-framed, mono-winged airplane in Waitohi.

March 31, 1921
- Great Britain declared a state of emergency because of the thousands of coal miners on strike.

March 31, 1992
- Sanctions are imposed on Libya by the UN after it refuses to hand over two men suspected of the bombing of Pan Am flight 103 over Lockerbie (22 December 1988).

March 31, 1960
- Under the recently declared state of emergency in South Africa (which followed the Sharpeville Massacre), 300 Black Africans are reported jailed and four more shot.

March 31, 1966
The Soviet Union launches Luna 10 which later becomes the first space probe to enter orbit around the Moon.

April 1, 1778
- Oliver Pollock, a New Orleans businessman, created the "$" symbol.

April 1, 1826
- Samuel Mory patented the internal combustion engine.

April 1, 1881
- Anti-Jewish riots took place in Jerusalem.

April 1, 1889
- The first dishwashing machine was marketed (in Chicago).

April 1, 1997
- In Nigeria, Government, bans forcible collection of tax by any tier of government and releases the approved list of taxes and levies.

DAYS OF HISTORY

April 1, 2004
- Vodacom Group and Econet Wireless Nigeria Limited announced a five-year Management Agreement.

April 1, 1924
- Adolf Hitler was sentenced to five years in prison for "Beer Hall Putsch." Gen Ludendorff was acquitted for leading the botched Nazi's "Beer Hall Putsch" in the German state of Bavaria

April 1, 1927
- The first automatic record changer was introduced by His Master's Voice.

April 1, 1947
- The 1st Jewish immigrants to Israel disembarked at Port of Elilat.

April 2, 1863
- Richmond Bread Riot: Food shortages incite hundreds of angry women to riot in Richmond, Virginia and demand that the Confederate government release emergency supplies.

April 2, 1870
- Victoria Claflin Woodhull (1838-1927) became the first woman to run for president of the United States when she announced her candidacy for the 1872 election, but she spent Election Day in jail for sending obscene literature through the mail. Woodhull was the first woman newspaper publisher, a feminist and a militant suffragist, but most shocking to Victorian sensibilities, she also advocated free love.

April 2, 1884
- The London prison for debtors closed.

April 2, 1917
- The first woman ever elected to the U.S. Congress, Jeeannette Rankin, takes her seat as a representative from Montana

April 2, 1963
- Reverend Dr. Martin Luther King began the first non-violent campaign in Birmingham, Alabama.

April 2, 1987
- IBM announced the upcoming release of the PS/2 and OS/2 computers featuring the Microsoft MS OS/2 and Windows 2.0 computer operating systems.

April 3, 1922
- Joseph Stalin succeeded Vladimir Lenin as leader of the Soviet Union.

April 3, 1944
- The U.S. Supreme Court ruled eight to one that
African Americans could not be barred from voting in the Texas Democratic primaries, stating that discrimination against blacks violated the 15th Amendment.

April 3, 1948
- President Harry S. Truman signed the European Recovery Programme, better known as the Marshall Plan, to stop the spread of Communism and restore the economic life of European countries devastated by World War II. Over four years, the programme distributed $12bn to the nations of Western Europe.

April 3, 1968
- Martin, Luther King Jnr. Delivered his "mountaintop" speech.

April 3, 1972
- The first ever Mobile phone call was placed by
Martin Cooper, in New York City.

April 3, 1986
- IBM unveiled the PC Convertible, their first laptop computer.

DAYS OF HISTORY

April 3, 1996
- An Air Force 737 carrying United States Secretary of Commerce, Ron Brown, crashed in Croatia, killing 35 of the 36 onboard, including Brown.

April 3, 1997
- Thalit massacre began in Algeria; all but one of the 53 inhabitants of Thalit were killed by guerrillas.

April 3, 1494
- Jamaica discovered by Christopher Columbus; he names it "St. Iago."

April 3, 1930
- Haile Selassie (Formally Ras Tafari) is proclaimed Emperor of Ethiopia.

April 3, 1937
- Gone with the Wind, a novel by Margaret Mitchell, wins the Pulitzer Prize for Fiction.

April 3, 1948
- The U.S. Supreme Court ruled that covenants prohibiting the sale of real estate to blacks and other minorities were legally unenforceable.

April 3, 1979
- Margaret Thatcher, leader of Britain's Conservative Party, won the general election to become the country's first female prime minister.

April 3, 1984
- One week after the death of Ahmed Sekou Toure in Guinea, Colonel Lansana Konte is declared president. Toure' prime minister, Louis Lansana Beavogui is removed as acting president by the military. with wide support from the public.

April 4, 1721
- Sir Robert Walpole enters office as the first Prime Minister of the United Kingdom under King George I.

April 4, 1887
- The first woman mayor was elected in the U.S. as Susanna M. Salter became mayor of Argonia, Kansas.

April 4, 1947
- U.N.'s International Civil Aviation Organization forms

April 4, 1949
- Twelve nations signed the treaty creating NATO, the North Atlantic Treaty. Organization. The nations united for common military defense against the threat of Soviet expansion in Western Europe.

April 4, 1968
- Civil Rights leader Rev. Dr. Martin Luther King was shot and killed by a sniper in Memphis, Tennessee. As head of the Southern Christian Leadership Conference, he championed non-violent resistance to end racial oppression and had been awarded the Nobel Peace Prize in 1964.

April 5, 1722
- Dutch explorer Jacob Roggeveen discovered Easter Island, a Polynesian Island 1400 miles from the coast of South America. Much of the population was later wiped out and the Island became a possession of Chile.

April 5, 1792
- George Washington cast the first presidential veto, rejecting a congressional measure for apportioning representatives among the states.

April 5, 1843
- Queen Victoria proclaimed Hong Kong a British crown colony.

April 5, 1930
- Mahatma Ghandi defied British law by making salt in India instead of buying it from the British.

42

DAYS OF HISTORY

April 5, 1965
- The second Indo-Pakistani conflict began when fighting broke out in the Rann of Kachchh, a sparsely inhabited region along the West Pakistan-India border.

April 5, 1968
- Riots erupted across the US following the Martin Luther King assassination.

April 5, 1974
- The World Trade Center (WTC), the tallest building in the world at 110 stories, opened in NYC.

April 5, 1992
- In Washington, D.C., a crowd estimated by authorities at half a million abortion rights.

April 6, 1941
- German bombardment on Piraeus (munitions ship explodes).

April 6, 1941
- Italian held Addis Ababa surrenders to British and Ethiopian forces.

April 6, 1939
- Great Britain and Poland sign military pact

April 6, 1939
- US and U.K. agree on joint control of Canton and
Enderbury Island in the Pacific

April 6, 1610
- Lailat-ul Qadar, night Koran descended to Earth

April 6, 1994
- The presidents of Rwanda and Burundi were killed in a plane crash.

April 6, 1896
- 1st modern Olympic games open in Athens Greece, American, James Connolly, wins 1st Olympic gold medal in mod history.

April 6, 1893
- Andy Bowen and Jack Burke box 7 hours 19minutes to no decision (111 rounds).

April 6, 1893
- Mormon Temple in Salt Lake City, Utah dedicated.

April 6, 1890
- French troops under captain Archinard occupy Segu, West-Sudan.

April 7, 1652
- The Dutch establish a settlement at Cape Town, South Africa.

April 7, 1902
- Texas Oil Company, Texaco, forms.

April 7, 1923
- First brain tumor operation under local anesthetic performed (Beth Israel Hospital in New York City) by Dr. K Winfield Ney.

April 7, 1940
- Booker T. Washington became the first black to be pictured on a U.S. postage stamp. His likeness was issued on a 10-cent stamp this day.

April 7, 1943
- Holocaust: In Terebovlia, Ukraine Germans order 1,100 Jews to undress to their underwear and march through the city of Terebovlia to the nearby village of Plebanivka where they are shot dead and buried in ditches.

April 7, 1948
- The World Health Organisation (WHO) established as a specialized agency of the United Nations (UN) that acts as a coordinating authority on international public health.

April 8, 1906
- Auguste Deter, the first person to be diagnosed with Alzheimer's disease, dies.

DAYS OF HISTORY

April 8, 1924
- Industrial Conciliation Act No 11 of 1924 introduces job reservation for whites in South Africa.

April 8, 1953
- Jomo Kenyatta the leader of the Kenya African Union Movement is sentenced to seven years hard labour for his part in the organization of the rebel Mau Mau movement.

April 8, 1963
- Mr Kenyatta took control as the first prime minister of a self governing Kenya and denied he was ever a member of the Mau Mau, his trial is generally regarded to have been rigged by the British because he was an advocate of self rule for Kenya and other African Nations.

April 8, 1946
- The last meeting of the League of Nations the Precursor of the United Nations, is held.

April 8, 1973
- Artist Pablo Picasso died.

April 8, 1979
- People's Republic of China joins ICC

April 8, 1992
- The satirical British magazine Punch publishes it's final issue on 8 April after 150 years due to falling sales and subscriptions.

April 9, 1866
- Despite a veto by President Andrew Johnson, the Civil Rights Bill of 1866 was passed by Congress granting blacks the rights and privileges of U.S. citizenship.

April 9, 1867
- Alaska purchase: Passing by a single vote, the United States Senate ratifies a treaty with Russia for the

April 9, 1872
- Samuel R. Percy patents dried milk.

April 9, 1937
- The kamikaze arrives at Croydon Airport in London- it is the first Japanese- built aircraft at fly to Europe.

April 9, 1960
- South African Prime Minister Hendrik Verwoerd is wounded in an attempted assassination by a disgruntled white by farmer, David Pratt, at the Rand Easter Show.

April 9, 1965
- The Mid-West Nigeria Legisature now has virtually a one-party system of the nine member of the Mid-West Democratic Front (MDF) to the ruling NCNC government.

April 9, 1992
- A US Federal Court finds former Panamanian dictator Manuel Noriega guilty of drug and racketeering charges. He is sentenced to 30 years in prison.

April 10, 1849
The safety pin was patented by Walter Hunt. in New York.

April 10, 1912
The RMS Titanic left port in Southampton, England for her
first and only voyage.

April 10, 1942
During World War II in the Pacific, the Bataan Death March began as American and Fillipino prisoners were forced on a six-day march from an airfield on Bataan to a camp near Cabanatuan. 76,000 Allied POWs including 12,000 Americans were forced to walk 60 miles under a blazing sun without food or water to the POW camp, resulting in over 5,000 American deaths.

DAYS OF HISTORY

April 1, 1970
- Paul McCartney announced the official split of the Beatles.

April 10, 1998
Politicians in Northem Ireland reached an agreement aimed at ending 30 years of violence which had claimed over 3,400 lives. Under the agreement, Protestants and Catholics in Northern Ireland would govern together in a new 108-member Belfast Assembly.

Birthday: Publisher Joseph Pulitzer (1847-1911) was born in Budapest, Hungary. He came to America in 1864 and later began a remarkable career in Journalism and publishing. His newspapers included the St. Louis Post-Dispatch and the New York World. He also endowed the journalism school at
Columbia University and established a fund for the Pulitzer Prizes, awarded annually for excellence in journalism.

April 11, 1909
- Albert Einstein introduces his Theory of Relativity.

April 11, 1919
- The International Labour Organization is founded.

April 11, 1961
- Adolf Eichmann, went on trial in an Israeli courthouse today, accused of mass murder and the helping in the death of millions of Jews in German
concentration Camps during World War II.

April 11, 1979
- Tanzanian backed rebels seize control in Uganda and the Uganda and the Uganda dictator Idi Amin is deposed as
President of Uganda and flees to Libya.

April 11, 1980
- Dr Canaan Sodindo Banana is selected as the first President of the newly independent Republic of Zimbabwe. He is officially inaugurated on 18 April.

April 11, 1983
- Harold Washington became the first African American Mayor of Chicago, receiving 51 per cent of the vote. Re-elected in 1987, he suffered a fatal heart attack at his office seven months later.

April 13, 1868
- Emperor Tewodros II of Ethiopia (also known as Thodore II) commits suicide as British troops under the command of Field Marshal Robert Napier storm the citadel at Magdala.

April 13, 1950
- Arab League signs a mutual defence treaty in Cairo.

April 13, 1964
- Ian Douglas Smith is named prime minister of Rhodesia by the while supremacist' Rhodesian Front party.

April 13, 1964
- At the Academy Awards, Sidney Poitier becomes the first African-American male to win the Best Actor award for Lilies of the Field.

April 13, 1968
- Biafra, a Nigerian province that has recently declared independence, is recognised by Tanzania the first nation to recognize its claimed new status.

April 13, 1975
- President Francois N'Garta Tombalbaye of Chad is killed during A military coup. After two days under interim head of state Noel Milarew Odingar, Felix Malloum N'Gakoutou takes power as
Chairman of the Higher Miltary Council.

DAYS OF HISTORY

April 13, 1994
- Prisdent guard at Kigali Rwanda, chops 1,200 church members to death.

April 14, 1828
- The first dictionary of American English was published by Noah Webster as the American Dictionary of the English Language.

April 14, 1865
- President Abraham Lincoln was shot and mortally wounded while watching a performance of Our American Cousin at Ford's Theater in Washington. He was taken to a nearby house and died the following morning at 7:22 a.m.

April 14, 1912
- The British passenger liner RMS Titanic hits an iceberg in the North Atlantic at 11:40pm. The ship sinks the following morning with the loss of 1,517 lives.

April 14, 1927
- The first Volvo car premieres in Gothenburg, Sweden.

April 14, 1956
- Ampex Corporation of Redwood City, CA demonstrated the first commercial magnetic tape recorder for sound and picture. The videotape machine had a price tag of $75,000. These early Ampex units were too large to fit in in a small room.

April 14, 1859
- Charles Dickens' "A Tale Of Two Cities" Published.

April 14, 1986
- Desmond Tutu elected Anglican archbishop of Capetown.

April 15, 1452
- Leonardo da Vinci (d. 1519), Italian painter, sculptor, Scientist and visionary, was born in Vinci near Florence.

April 16, 1969
- The text of the Lusaka Manifesto is agreed by leaders of East and Central African states at the end of the Lusaka summit. The manifesto states that "all men are equal, and have equal rights to human dignity and respect, regardless of colour, race, religion or sex."

April 16, 1977
- Alex Haley finds his Roots in Juffure, Gambia

April 16, 1995
- Iqbal Masih, the young boy from Pakistan who spoke out against child labor, was shot to death.

April 17. 1397
Geoffrey Chaucer tells the Canterbury Tales for the first time at the court of Richard II. Chaucer scholars have also identified this date (in 1387) as the start of the book's pilgrimage to Canterbury.

April 17, 1958
The South African National Party won a third successive General election allowing further introductions of 'Grand Apartheid' legislation.

April 17, 1961
Bay of Pigs Invasion: A group of CIA financed and trained Cuban refuges landed at the Bay of Pigs in Cuba with the aim of ousting Fidel Castro.

April 17, 1964
Geraldine Mock became the first woman to fly solo around the world.

April 17, 1971
Sierra Leone became a republic.

DAYS OF HISTORY

April 17, 1989
The Polish Labour Union Solidarity was granted legal Status after nearly a decade of struggle, paving the way for the downfall of the Polish Communist Party. In the elections that followed, Solidarity government led by Lech Walesa.

Birthday: American financier, John Pierpont (J.P) Morgan (1837-1913), was born in Hartford, Connecticut. He developed extraordinary management skills, reorganizing
and consolidating a number of failing companies to make them profitable. His extensive interests included banking, steel,
railroads and art collecting. In 1895, he aided the failing U.S. Treasury by carrying out a private bond sale among fellow financiers to replenish the treasury.

April 18, 1902
- Denmark is first country to adopt fingerprinting to identify criminals

April 18, 1924
- Simon & Schuster publishes the first Crossword puzzle book.

April 18, 1946
- The League of Nations is dissolved.

April 18, 1948
- International Court of Justice opens at Hague Netherlands.

April 18, 1954
- Colonel Gamal Abdal Nasser seizes power and becomes Prime Minister of Egypt.

April 18, 1955
- Celebrated physicist and Nobel Laureate Albert Einstein died today at the age of 76.

April 18, 1977
- Alex Haley, author of "Roots," awarded Pulitzer Prize.

April 18, 1980
- Zimbabwe (formerly Rhodesia) proclaimed an independent Republic. Dr Cannan Sodindo Banana is inaugurated as president, and Robert Gabriel Mugabe as prime minister.

April 19, 1713
- With no living male heirs, Charles VI, Holy Roman Emperor, issues the Pragmatic Sanction of 1713 to ensure that Habsburg lands and the Austrian throne would be inherited by his daughter, Maria Theresa of Austria (not actually born until 1717).

April 19, 1782
- John Adams secures the Dutch Republic's recognition of the United States as an independent government. The house which he had purchased in The Hague, Netherlands becomes the first American embassy.

April 19, 1809
- An Austrian corps is defeated by the forces of the Duchy of Warsaw in the Battle of Raszyn, part of the struggles of the Fifth Coalition. On the same day the Austrian main army is defeated by a First French Empire Corps led by Louis Nicolas Davout at the Battle of Teugen-Hausen in Bavaria; part of a four day campaign which ended in a French victory.

April 19, 1810
- Venezuela achieves home rule: Vicenta Emparan, Governor of the Captaincy General is removed by the people of Caracas and a Junta is installed.

April 20, 1841
- The first detective story, Edgar Allen Poe's Murders in the Rue Morgue was published.

April 20, 1853
- Harriet Tubman starts the Underground Railroad, a clandestine organization to smuggle slaves to freedom.

DAYS OF HISTORY

April 20, 1862
- Louis Pasteur and Claude Bernard complete the first pasteurization tests.

April 20, 1902
- Marie and Pierre Curie isolate the radioactive element radium.

April 20, 1940
- First election microscope demonstrated (RCA), Philadelphia Trial, Nelson Mandela says it is in response to the South African Government's Apartheid policies that African nationalist leaders have resorted to violence.

April 20, 1979
- Egyptian president Muhammad Anwar al-Sadat gets an overwhelming majority in a vote for peace treaty with Isreal.

April 21, 1948
1st Polaroid camera was sold in U.S.

April 21, 1859
- David Livingstone arrives at Cape Town on the start of his expedition through the interior of Africa.

April 21, 1945
- Russian troops capture some outlying suburbs of Berlin at the beginning of what promises to be a bitter battle for control of the city.

April 21, 1975
- The President of South Vietnam (President Thieu) resigns accusing the United States of betrayal in a blistering attack broadcast to the nation.

April 21, 1998
- Astronomers announced in Washington they had discovered possible signs of a new family of planets orbiting a star 220 light-years away, the clearest evidence yet of worlds forming beyond our solar system. The dust structures were thought to be new solar systems forming around 3 sun-

April 21, 1994
- One of the Guildford Four, Paul Hill, has won his appeal against a conviction for an IRA murder in Northern Ireland.

April 22, 1864
- The U.S. Congress passes the Coinage Act of 1864 which mandates that the inscription "In God We Trust" be United States currency.

April 22, 1969
- Doctors at Methodist Hospital in Houston performed what was billed as the first human eye transplant on John Madden, 54, owner of a photography studio.

April 22, 1970
- The first celebration of Earth Day was on April 22, 1970. Day was on April 22, 1970. The annual event has become the largest Organized demonstration in history with more than 20 million participants World-wide. In history effort to keep environmental issues at the forefront of the community.

April 22, 1980
- Thirteen ministers of the ousted government (William Richard Tolbert's True Whig party) in Liberia are executed by order of the 'Redemption Council' of Sergeant Samule Kanyon Doe's ruling military regime.

April 23, 1564
- William Shakespeare was born at Stratford-on-Avon in England. Renowned as the most influential writer in the English language, he created 36 plays and 154 Sonnets, including Romeo and Juliet, Hamlet and The Merchant of Venice. Died April 23, 1616.

DAYS OF HISTORY

April 23, 1956
- U.S. Supreme Court ends race segregation on buses 1969 Sirhan Sirhan was sentenced to death (later reduced to a life sentence) for the assassination of Robert F. Kennedy a Democratic Senator from New York.

April 23, 1984
- Singer Marvin Gaye the Motown singer who had numerous hits including "I Heard it Through the Grapevine" was shot to death by his father at age 45. His father was suffering from a brain tumor at the time and after pleading guilty to manslaughter was sentenced to six years of probation.

April 24, 1800
- The United States Library of Congress was established when President John Adams signed legislation to appropriate $5,000 to purchase "such books as may be necessary for the use of Congress."

April 24, 1915
- In Asia Minor during World War I, the first modern-era genocide began with the deportation of Armeniah leaders from Constantinople and subsequent massacre by Young Turks. In May, deportations of all Armenians and mass murder by Turks began, resulting in the complete elimination of the Armenians from the Ottoman Empire and all of the historic Armenian homelands. Estimates vary from 800.000 to over 2,000,000 Armenians murdered.

April 24, 1970
- The Gambia became a Republic within the Commonwealth of Nations, with Dawda Jawara as the first President.

April 24, 1980
- The mission to rescue the 52 hostages from the US embassy in Iran (Operation Eagle Claw) was aborted due to equipment failure.

The Iranian foreign minister warned that any attempt by the US would be considered an act of war. Eight US Servicemen lost their lives in the aborted attempt.

April 24, 1993
- Death of Oliver Tambo (born 1917): South African political leader, co-founder of the ANC's Youth League, and president of the ANC from 1980 to 1991.

April 24, 2005
- Cardinal Joseph Ratzinger was inaugurated as the 265th Pope of the Roman Catholic Church taking the name Pope Benedict XVI.

April 25, 1616
- English post and dramatist William Shakespeare, 52, died on what has been traditionally regarded as the anniversary of his birth in 1564.

April 25, 1896
The Vitascope system for projecting movies onto a screen was publicly demonstrated in New York City.

April 25, 1901
New York became the first state to require license plates on cars

April 25, 1915
- World War I The Battle of Gallipoli begins- The invasion of the Turkish Gallipoli Peninsula by Australian, British, French and New Zealand troops begins with landings at Anzac Cove and Cape Helles.

April 25, 1944
- The United Negro College Fund is incorporated.

April 25, 1945
- Fifty nations gather in San Francisco, California to begin the United Nations Conference on International Organizations.

DAYS OF HISTORY

April 25, 1961:
- Robert Noyce is granted a patent for an integrated circuit.

April 26, 1933
- The Gestapo, the official secret police force of Nazi Germany, is established.
1964   The African nations of Tanganyika and Zanzibar merged to form Tanzania.

April 26, 1970
- The Convention Establishing the World Intellectual Property Organisation enters into force.

April 26, 1986
- The world's worst nuclear accident occurred in Pripyat, Ukraine, north of Kiev, at 1:23 a.m. as the Chermobyi atomic power plant exploded. A 300-hundred-square-mile area was evacuated and 31 people died as unknown thousands were exposed to radioactive material that spread in the atmosphere throughout the world.

April 26, 1994
- Multiracial elections were held for the first time in the history of South Africa. With approximately 18million blacks voting, Nelson Mandela was elected president and F.W. de Klerk vice president.

April 27, 1950
- Apartheid: In South Africa, the Group Areas Act is passed formally segregating races.

April 27, 1956
- Rocky Marciano retired as undefeated world heavyweight boxing champion.

April 27, 1961
- Sierra Leone is granted its independence from the United Kingdom, with Milton Margai as the first Prime Minister.

April 27, 1965
- RC Duncan patents "Pampers" disposable diaper.

April 27, 1976
- Arabic Monetary Fund established in Abu Dhabi

April 27, 1992
- Betty Boothroyd becomes the first woman to be elected Speaker of the British House of Commons in its 700-year history.

April 27, 1993
- All members of the Zambia national football team lose their lives in a plane crash off Libreville, Gabon en route to Dakar, Senegal to play a 1994 FIFA World Cup qualifying match against Senegal.

April 28, 1916
- Ferruccio Lamborghini, (Born 28 Apr 1916; died 20 Feb 1993), Italian Industrialist who founded a luxury car company that produced some of the fastest, most expensive, and sought-after spots cars in the world.

April 28, 1932
- A vaccine for yellow fever is announced for use on humans.

April 28, 1945
- Twenty three years of Fascist rule in Italy abruptly ended as Italian partisans executed Benito Mussolini. Other leaders of the Fascist Party and friends of Mussolini were also killed along with his mistress, Clara Petacci.

April 28, 1967
Muhammad Ali refuses induction into United States army and stripped of boxing title.

April 28, 1969
- The French President Charles de Gaulle, resigns from President of France after 11 years, following his defeat in a referendum

DAYS OF HISTORY

April 29, 1852
- First edition of Peter Roget's Thesaurus published.

April 29, 1813
- A patent for rubber was given to J.F. Hummel of Philadelphia. PA.

April 29, 1845
- Macon B. Allen and Robert Morris Jr, the first recorded Blacks to practice law, (open practice) in the United States.

April 29, 1913
- Swedish engineer Gideon Sundback of Hoboken patents all-purpose zipper.

April 29, 1963
- The Federal Prime Minister of Nigeria, Sir Abubakar Tafawa Balewa, announced that Nigeria would become a republic within the Commonwealth by October 1963.

April 29, 1992
- In Los Angeles, California four white Los Angeles police officers that had been caught beating an unarmed African-American motorist in an amateur video are acquitted of any wrongdoing in the arrest.

April 30, 1789
- On the balcony of Federal Hall on Wall Street in New York City, George Washington takes the oath of office to become the first elected President of the United States.

April 30, 1945
- On this day in 1945, holed up in a bunker under his headquarters in Berlin, Adolf Hitler commits suicide by swallowing a cyanide capsule and shooting himself in the head. Soon after, Germany unconditionally surrendered to the Allied forces, ending Hitler's dreams of a 1,000-years Reich.

April 30, 1948
- Palestiniah Jews declared their independence from British rule and established the new state of Isreal. The country became a destination for tens of thousands of Nazi Holocaust survivors and a strong U.S ally.

May 1
- Observed as May Day, a holiday and Spring festival since ancient times. It became since ancient times. It became a Workers' Day in the U.S. in the 1880s and was also observed in Socialist countries as a worker' holiday or Labour Day.

May 1, 1328
- Wars of Scottish Independence ended and Treaty of Edinburgh-Northampton was signed,with the Kingdom of England recognizing the Kingdom of Scotland as an independence state.

May 1, 1707
- Great Britain was founded from a union between England and Scotland. The union included Wales which had already been part of England since the 1500s. The UK today consists of Great Britain and Northern Ireland.

May 1, 1834
- The British colonies abolished slavery.

May 1, 1925
- The All-China Federation of Trade Unions was officially founded. Today, it is the largest trade union in the world, with 134 million members.

May 1, 1927
- The first cooked meals on a scheduled flight were Introduced on an Imperial Airways flight from London to Paris.

DAYS OF HISTORY

May 1, 1945
- World War II: A German newsreader officially announced that Adolf Hitler had "fallen at his command post in the Reich Chancellery fighting to the last breath against Bolshevism and for Germany."

May 1, 1961
- The Prime Minister of Cuba, Fidel Castro, Proclaimed Cuba a socialist nation and abolished elections.

May 1, 2004
- Eight former Communist nations and two Mediterranean countries joined the European Union, marking its largest-ever expansion.

May 2, 1598
- Henry IV signed the Treaty of Vervins, ending Spain's interference in France.

May 2, 1776
- France and Spain agreed to donate arms to American rebels.

May 2, 1919
- The first U.S. air passenger service started.

May 2, 1923
- Lieutenants Okaley Kelly and John Macready took off from New York for the West Coast on what would become the first successful nonstop transcontinental flight.

May 2, 1934
- Nazi Germany began "People's court."

May 2, 1956
- US Methodist church disallowed race separation.

May 2, 1980
- Pope John Paul II arrived Kinshasa for the centennial of Catholicism in Zaire and the beginning of his African tour.

May 4, 1799
- Fourth Anglo-Mysore War: The Battle of Seringapatam ends when the city is assaulted and the Tipu Sultan killed by the besieging British army, under the command of General George Harris.

May 4, 1799 1814
- Emperor Napoleon I of France arrives at Portoferraio on the island of Elba to begin his exile.

May 4, 1814
- King Ferdinand VII of Spain signs the Decrete of the 4th of May, returning Spain to absolutism.

May 4, 1855
- American adventurer William Walker departs from San Francisco with about 60 men to conquer Nicaragua.

May 4, 1859
- The Cornwall Railway opens across the Royal Albert Bridge linking the counties of Devon and Cornwall in England.

May 4, 1942
- World War II: The Battle of the Coral Sea begins with an attack by aircraft from the United States aircraft carrier USS Yorktown on Japanese naval forces at Tulagi Island in the Solomon Islands. The Japanese forces had invaded Tulagi the day before.

May 5, 1818
- Founder of modern Communism Karl Marx was born in Treves, Germany. He co-authored Das Kapital and The Communist Manifesto, advocating the abolition of all private property and a system in which workers own all the means of production, land, factories and machinery. (Died 1883).

DAYS OF HISTORY

May 5, 1925
- The government of South Africa declares Afrikaans an official language.

May 5, 1925
- A high school science teacher John scopes was arrested for teaching evolution in one of Tennessee's public schools in violation of the Butler Act.

May 5, 1999
- After 20 years of military rule, the Head of State, General Abdulsalami Abubakar, moved Nigeria closer to democracy with the promulgation of the decree which gives a legal effect to the new 1999 constitution.

May 6, 1835
- James Gordon Bennett, Sr. publishes the first issue of the New York Herald.

May 6, 1851
- Dr. John Gorrie patents a "refrigeration machine."

May 6, 1954
- Roger Bannister becomes the first person to run the mile in under four minutes.

May 6, 1856
- Founder of psychoanalysis Sigmund Freud was born in Freiberg, Moravia. His theories became the foundation for treating psychiatric disorders by psychoanalysis and offered some of the first workable cures for mental disorders. (Died 1939).

May 6, 1997
- The Chancellor, Gordon Brown, gives the Bank of England Independence from political control.

May 6, 1990
- Former president PW Botha quit South Africa's ruling National Party.

May 6, 2000
- Conjunction of Sun, Mercury, Venus, Mars, Jupiter, Saturn & Moon.

May 7, 1399BC
- Socrates (b.469BC), Greek philosopher, committed Suicide. He had been indicted for rejecting the Gods acknowledged by the State, of bringing in strange deities, and of corrupting the youth.

May 7, 1873
- Jose Antonio Paez Head of State and First President of Venezuela dies. 1888- George Eastman patented his Kodak box camera.

May 7, 1913
- British House of Commons rejected women's right to vote.

May 7, 1999
- In Guinea-Bissau renegade troops forced the surrender of the 600-man presidential guard and ousted President Joao Bernardo Vieira, who sought refuge in the Portuguese Embassy.

May 7, 2000
- Presidency invites Ooni of Ife Oba Okunade Sijuwade and Ogunsua of Modakeke, Oba Francis Adedoyin over Ife/Modakeke crisis.

May 9, 1927
- Canberra replaces Melbourne as the capital of Australia.

May 9, 1936
- Five days after Italy captured the Ethiopian capital of Addis Ababa, Mussolini announces that Abyssinian is now part of the Italian Empire.

DAYS OF HISTORY

May 9, 1955
- Cold War: West German joins NATO.

May 9, 1994
- South Africa's newly elected parliament chose Nelson Mandela to be the country's first black president. Mandela promised a South Africa for "all its people, black and white."

May 9, 1995
- Kinshasa, capital of Zaire (later Congo), was Placed under quarantine after an outbreak of the Ebola virus.

May 9, 1999
- In East Timor violence in Dili between separatists and anti-independence militia began and left 4 people dead over the next 2 days.

May 10, 1655
- England, with troops under the command of Admiral William Penn and General Robert Venables, annexes Jamaica from Spain.

May 10, 1872
- Victoria Woodhull became the first woman nominated for U.S. President. Frederick Douglas, African-American statesman, was nominated as vice president on the Equal Rights Party Virginia.

May 10, 1908
- Mother's Day is observed for the first time in the United States, in Grafton, West Virgina.

May 10, 1940
- Winston Churhill took office as PM. Churchill formed a new government and served as the Conservative head of a coalition government with the opposition Labor Party. The debate over the Norway campaign led directly to Churchill replacing Chamberlain.

May 11, 1812
- Prime Minister Spencer Perceval is assassinated by John Bellingham in the lobby of the House of Commons, London.

May 11, 1924
- Mercedes-Benz is formed by Gottlieb Daimler and Kari Benz merging their two companies.

May 11, 1960
- In Buenos Aires, Argentina, four Isreali Mossad agents Capture fugitive Nazi Adolf Eichmann, living under the assumed name Ricardo Klement.

May 11, 1956
- The Gold Coast / Ghana becomes the first black African nation to be granted independence from Britain.

May 12, 1820
- English nurse and public health activist Florence Nightingale was born in Florence. Italy. She volunteered to aid British troops in Turkey where she improved hospital sanitary conditions and greatly reduced the death rate for wounded and sick soldiers. (Died Aug 13, 1910)

May 12, 1910
- Dorothy Mary Crowfoot Hodgkin was born. Hodgkin was a British chemist who pioneered 3 dimensional x-ray crystallography of molecules. She used this technique to discover the structure of many important biochemicals such as penicillin, vitamin B12 insulin.

May 12. 1942
- Holocaust: 1,500 Jew are sent to gas chambers in Auschwitz.

May 13, 1890
- Lord Salisbury offers Germany Helgoland in exchange for Zanzibar, Uganda and Equatoria.

DAYS OF HISTORY

May 13, 1949
- First British-produced jet bomber, Canberra, makes its first test flight.

May 13, 1960
- With Patrice Lumumba (Congolese nationalist) still under arrest, fighting has broken out between rival congolese tribes in the streets of the capital Kinshasa.

May 13, 1981
- Pope John Paul II was shot and wounded by Mehmet Ali Agca as he drove through a crowd in St. Peter's Square, Rome.

May 14, 1686
- German physicist Gabriel Fahrenheit was born in Danzig, Germany. He introduced the use of mercury in thermometers and greatly improved their accuracy. His name is now attached to one of the major temperature Measurement scales (Dies 1736).

May 14, 1796
- Smallpox vaccine was developed by Dr. Edward Jenner, A physician in rural England. He coined the term vaccination for the new procedure of injecting a milder form of the disease into a healthy persons resulting in immunity.

May 14, 1878
- The trademarked name Vaseline (for a brand of petroleum jelly) was registered by Robert A. Chesebrough.

May 15, 1930
- On a Boeing Air Transport flight between Oakland and Chicago, Ellen Church became the first airline stewardess.

May 15, 1970
- President Richard Nixon appointed Anna Mae Hays and Elizabeth P. Hoisington the first female United States Army Generals.

May 15, 1972
- George Wallace was shot while campaigning for the U.S. presidency in Laurel, Maryland. As a result, Wallace was permanently paralyzed from the waist down.

May 15, 1985
- Prince Michael of Moldavia and Amanda Carrington tied the knot in wedded bliss on the right-time soap opera. 'Dynasty.' The series was cancelled shortly after the wedding and Joan Collins says she hasn't gotten a letter or anything from the couple.

May 15, 1988
- Soviet war in Afghanistan: After more than eight years of fighting, the Soviet Union began to withdraw its estimated 115,000 troops from Afghanistan.

May 16, 1907
- Nairobi is selected to be the capital of British East Africa.

May 16, 1918
- The Sedition Act of 1918 is passed by the U.S. Congress, Making criticism of the government an imprisonable offense.

May 16, 1948
- Chaim Weizmann is elected the first President of Israel.

May 16, 1963
- Chief Anthony Enahoro was flown from London to Lagos. He was charged with treasonable felony. About 60 policemen were at Ikeja Airport to control a crowd of several hundred people, who, whoever never saw Chief Enahoro, as he was smuggled out in a Nigeria Airways catering van.

May 16, 1975
- Japanese Junko Tabei became first woman to reach Mount Everest's summit.

DAYS OF HISTORY

May 16, 1997
- President Mobutu Sese Seko of Zaire ended 32 years of Autocratic rule when rebel forces led by Laurent Kabila expelled him from the country.

May 17, 1792
- Stock traders signed the Buttonwood Agreement in New York City. Where business had been transacted in the past. 24 merchants formed their exchange at Wall and Water Streets where they fixed rates on commissions on stocks and bonds.

May 17, 1814
- Denmark ceded Norway to Sweden. Norway's constitution Was signed providing for a limited monarchy.

May 17, 1900
- Ayatollah Ruhollah Khomeini (d.1989), Iran's spiritual and revolutionary leader (1979-89), was born.

May 17, 1902
- Greek archaeologist Valerios Stais discovers the Antikythera mechanism, an ancient mechanical analog computer.

May 18, 1642
- The Canadian city of Montreal was founded by French colonists.

May 18, 1652
- Rhode Island passes the first law in North America making slavery illegal.

May 18, 1896
- The US Supreme Court ruled 7 to 1 to give states The authority to segregate people according to race.

May 18, 1920
- People John Paul II was born as Karol Jozef Wojtyla, in Wadowice, Poland.

In 1978 he became the 26th Roman Catholic pope. He was the first non-Italian Roman. Catholic pope since the Renaissance and wrote the international bestseller "Crossing the Threshold" (Died 2005).

May 19, 1780
- New England's Dark Day: A combination of thick smoke
and heavy cloud cover causes complete darkness to fall on Eastern Canada and the New England area of the United States at 10:30 A.M.

May 19, 1795
- Johns Hopkins, founder of Johns Hopkins University, was born.

May 19, 1885
- German chancellor Bismarck took possession of Cameroon & Togoland.

May 19, 1967
- The Soviet Union ratified a treaty with the United States and Britain banning nuclear weapons from outer space.

May 19, 1991
- Martial-law courts in Kuwait began trying people accused of collaborating with Iraqi occupation forces, sentencing one man to life in prison for wearing a saddam Hussein T-shirt.

May 20, 1570
- Cartographer Abraham Ortelius issues the first modern atlas.

May 20, 1802
- By the Law, Napoleon Bonaparte reinstates slavery in the French colonies. revoking its abolition in the French Revolution.

May 20, 1867
- British parliament rejected John Stuart Mill's law on women suffrage.

DAYS OF HISTORY

May 20, 1902
Cuba gains independence from the United States. Tomas Estrada Palma becomes the first President of Cuba.

May 20, 1927
- By the Treaty of Jedda, the United Kingdom recognizes the sovereignty of King Ibn Saud in the Kingdoms of Hejaz and Nejd, which later merge to become the Kingdom of
Saudi Arabia.

May 21, 1891
- Boxes Peter Jackson and Jim Corbett fight to a draw in 61 rounds.

May 21, 1904
- The Federation Internationale de Football Association (FIFA) is founded in Paris.

May 21, 1946
- Physicist Louis Slotin is fatally irradiated in a critically Incident during an experiment the Demon core at Los Alamos National Laboratory.

May 21, 1956
- The first hydrogen bomb to be dropped by air exploded over the Bikini Atoll in the Pacific.

May 21, 1991
- The prime minister of India from 1984 until 1989, Rajiv Gandhi was in the midst of a campaign rally for reelection when a bomb exploded in his hand.

May 22, 1570
-First atlas with 70maps was published May 22, 1892 Dr. Washington Sheffield invented toothpaste tube

May 22, 1906
- The Wright brothers were granted U.S. patent number 821, 393 for their "Flying Machine," the aeroplane.

May 22, 1945
- Winston Churchill resigned as Prime Minister of England which brought an end to the coalition cabinet formed during the war.

May 22, 1947
- Congress approved the Truman Doctrine, assuring U.S. Support for Greece and Turkey to prevent the spread of Communism.

May 22, 1963
- Mr. Kenneth Potter, junior counsel to Mr. Foot, QC, was granted permission to enter Nigeria to defend Chief Anthony Enahoro, charged with treasonable felony, conspiracy to commit and unlawful importing and possession of arms and ammunition at the High Court, Lagos.

May 22, 1972
- Ceylon adopted a new constitution, became a Republic, changed its name to Sri lanka, and joined the Commonwealth of Nations.

May 22, 1972
- Richard Nixon became the first American President to visit Moscow, Four days later, Nixon and Soviet leader, Leonid Brezhnev, signed a pact pledging to freeze nuclear arsenals at current levels.

May 23, 1829
- Accordion patent granted to Cyrill Demian in Vienna.

May 23, 1900
- Association Press News Service forms in New York.

May 23, 1934
- Wallace Carothers manufactures first nylon (polymer 66)

DAYS OF HISTORY

May 23, 1945
- Heinrich Himmler, head of Adolf Hitler's Gestapo, committed suicide while in prison.

May 23, 1949
- The Federal Republic of Germany is established and the Basic Law for the Federal Republic of Germany is proclaimed.

May 23, 1937
- John D. Rockefella the American industrialist once the worlds richest man before he gave his millions away has died at 97 yrs old, he went from a $4.50 clerk to the world's richest man only to give most of it away in the last 30 years for philanthropic deeds.

May 24, 1738
- John Wesley is converted, essentially launching the Methodist Movement; the day is celebrated annually by Methodists as Aldersgate Day. The Methodist Church was established.

May 24, 1883
- The Brooklyn Bridge, hailed as the "eighth wonder of the world," was dedicated by President Chester Arthur and New York Gov. Grover Cleveland, and officially opened to traffic.

May 24, 1966
- General Aguiyi Ironsi proclaims Unification Decree 34. It abolished the regions, divided the country into 35 provinces and unified the federal and regional public services under a single Public Service Commission in Nigeria.

May 25, 1765
- The Gambia was made a part of the British colony of SeneGambia with its headquarters at St. Louis.

May 25, 1946
- Transjordan (now Jordan) gained independence from Britain and become a kingdom as it proclaimed its new Monarch, King Abdullah Ibn Ul-Hussein.

May 25, 1963
- In Addis Ababa, Ethiopia, the Organisation of African Unity is established.

May 25, 1975
- ECOWAS Treaty 1 was signed. The Economic Community of West African States (ECOWAS) was formed in Nigeria with 15 members that included: Benin, Burkina Faso, Cape Verde, Coted'Ivoire, Gambia, Ghana, Guinea, Guinea-Bissau, Liberia, Mali, Niger, Nigeria, Senegal, Sierra Leone, and Togo.

May 26, 1897
- The vampire novel Dracula, by Irish writer Bram Stoker, Goes on sale in London bookshops.

May 26, 1918
- The Democratic Republic of Georgia is established.

May 26, 1937
- Egypt joins the League of Nations as its 59th member.

May 26, 1943
- First president of a black country to visit US (Edwin Barclay, Liberia)

May 26, 1957
- The Algerian vice-president, Ali Chekkal, is assassinated by Algerian Nationalists whilst attending the French football cup final.

May 26, 2003
- Rwandans voted to approve a new constitution that instituted a balance of power between Hutu and Tutsi.

DAYS OF HISTORY

May 27, 1679
- Habeaus Corpus Act (no false arrest and imprisonment) passed in UK

May 27, 1943
- The Ballpoint pen, is patented in America by Hungarian Laszio Biro,

May 27, 1963
- The Judicial Committee of the Privy Council gave its judgment. The Council held that Chief Akintola's dismissal by the Governor, Sir Adesoji Aderemi was valid thereby maintaining Alhaji Adegbenro's claim to premiership of Western Region.

May 27, 1963
- The Kenya African Nation Union, wins the country's first general election and the leader of the party Jomo Kenyatta becomes Kenya's first prime minister.

May 28, 1664
- First Baptist Church organizes (Boston).

May 28, 1952
- The women of Greece are given the right to vote.

May 28, 1961
- Amnesty International was founded by London lawyer Peter Berenson. He read about the arrest of a group of students in Portugal then launched a one-year campaign to free them called Appeal for Amnesty. Today Amnesty International has over a million members in 150 countries working to free prisoners of conscience, stop torture and the death penalty, and guarantee human rights for women.

May 28, 1964
- The Palestine Liberation Organization is formed.

May 28, 1991
- The Ethiopian People's Revolutionary Democratic Front (EPRDF) take control of the nation's capitol Addis Ababa ending 17 years of Marxist rule in Ethiopia.

May 29, 1453
- The city of Constantinople was captured by the Turks. Who renamed it Istanbul. This marked the end of the Byzantine Empire as Istanbul became the capital of the Ottoman Empire.

May 29, 1917
- John Fitzgerald Kennedy, the 35th President of the United States of America (1961-1963), was born at 83 Beals St. In Brookline, Mass. He was assassinated in his first term.

May 29, 1953
- Mount Everest was conquered as Edmund Hillary of New Zealand and Tensing Norgay, a Serpa of Nepal, became the first climbers to reach the summit. Norgay later authored the autobiography "Man of Everest."

May 29, 1962
- Federal Government of Nigeria declared a state of emergency in Western Nigeria with Dr. Moses Majekodunmi as Sole Administrator following intra-party and parliamentary crisis Involving members of the Action Group.

May 29, 1968
- Manchester United beat Portuguese side, Benfica, 4-1 to become the first English club to win the European Cup.
The Manchester United team included the legendary George Best, who named European Footballer of the Year.

May 29, 1999
- Commonwealth heads of government lifted Nigeria's suspension imposed in 1995, from the organization.

May 29, 1999
- Olusegun Obasanjo was sworn-in as Nigeria's democratically elected President after 15 years of military rule.

DAYS OF HISTORY

May 30, 1783
- The Pennsylvania Evening Post by Benjamin Towne in Philadelphia, became the first daily newspaper published in America.

May 30, 1821
- James Boyd patents Rubber Fire Hose

May 30, 1848
- W.G. Young of Baltimore, MD patented the ice-cream freezer just in time for spring and summer treats!

May 30, 1909
- The National Conference on the Negro opens, leading to the founding of the National Association for the Advancement of Coloured people (NAACP).

May 30, 1966
- Former Congolese Prime Minister Evariste Kimba and several other politicians are publicity executed in Kinshasa on the orders of President Joseph Mobutu.

May 31, 1279
- BC Rameses II (The Great) (19th dynasty) becomes pharaoh of Ancient Egypt.

May 31, 1790
- The United States enacts its first copyright statute, the Copyright Act of 1790.

May 31, 1898
- Norman Vincent Peale (d1993), American religious leader, was born in Ohio. He later authored "The Power of Positive Thinking."

May 31, 1909
- The National Association for the Advancement of Colored People (NAACP) held its first conference at the United Charities Building in NYC.

May 31, 1961
- Republic of South Africa created.

May 31, 1979
- Zimbabwe proclaimed its independence.

June 1, 1943
- British Overseas Airways Corporation Flight 777 is shot down over the Bay of Biscay by German Junkers Ju 88s, killing actor Leslie Howard.

June 1, 1980
- Cable News Network (CNN) begins broadcasting.

June 1, 1990
- George H. W. Bush and Mikhail Gorbachev sign a treaty to end chemical weapon production.

June 1, 1968
- The Famous blind and deaf author Helen Keller whobecame a world-famous speaker, Political Activist and author, Helen Keller, dies.

June 1, 1923
- Both Great Britain and the United States are demanding
back the loans made to France borrowed during the First
World War.

June 1, 1933
- The aviator, Roger Williams, announces his plans to fly a round-trip flight across the Atlantic ocean.

June 2, 1924
- U.S. President Calvin Coolidge signs the Indian Citizenship Act into law, granting citizenship to all Native Americans born within the territorial limits of the United States.

DAYS OF HISTORY

June 2, 1946
- Birth of the Italians Republic: In a referendum, Italians vote to turn Italy from a monarchy into a Republic.

June 2, 1953
- The coronation of Queen Elizabeth II, who was crowned Queen of the United Kingdom, Canada, Australia, New Zealand and Her Other Realms and Territories & Head of the Commonwealth, the first major international event to be televised.

June 2, 1993
- South Africa's Supreme Court upheld Winnie Mandela's Conviction for kidnapping four young blacks, but said she would not have to serve her five-year prison term.

June 4, 1973
- A patent for the ATM is granted to Donald Wetzel, Tom Bames and George Chastain.

June 4, 1979
- Flight Lieutenant Jerry Rawlings takes power in Ghana after a military coup in which General Fred Akuffo is overthrown.

June 4, 1989
- The Chinese government ordered its troops to open fire on unarmed protesters in Tiananmen Square in Beijing. Armored personnel carries then rolled into the square crushing students still sleeping in their tents.

June 4, 1999
- Governor of Lagos State, Bola Tinubu, renames Louis Farrakhan Crescent (formerly Eleke Crescent) ater Walter Carrington, former US Ambassador to Nigeria; Kingsway Road after Pa Alfred Rewane and Oregun Road after Kudirat Abiola.

June 5, 1783
- The first sustained flight occurred as a hot-air balloon was launched at Annonay, France, by brothers Joseph and Jacques Montgolfier. Their 33-foot diameter globe aerostatique ascended about 6,000 feet.

June 5, 1794
- Congress passed the Neutrality Act, which prohibits Americans from enlisting in the service of a foreign power.

June 5, 1959
- The first government of the State of Singapore was sworn in.

June 5, 1967
- Six-Day War began: The Israeli air force launched simultaneous attacks on Egypt, Syria, Jordan and Iraq Jordan lost the West Bank.

Birthday
Scottish economist and philosopher, Adam Smith (1723-1790), was born in Kirkcaldy, Scotland, He wrote An Enquiry into the Nature and Causes of the Wealth of Nations, published in 1776. The book described the workings of a market economy And established him as one of the most influential of modern economic theory.

Birthday British economist, John Maynard Keynes (1883-1946), was born in Cambridge, England, He wrote The General Theory of Employment, Interest and Money in 1936, stating his ideals about government responsibility and commitment to maintaining high employment. He claimed that investors and governments, not consumers, were the source of business cycle shifts.

June 6, 1716
- The 1st slaves arrived in Louisiana.

DAYS OF HISTORY

June 6, 1809
- Sweden promulgates a new Constitution. Which restores political power to the Riksdag of the Estates after 20 years of Enlightened absolutism. It declared independence and a constitutional monarchy is established.

June 6, 1833
- U.S. President Andrew Jackson becomes the first President to ride a train.

June 6, 1844
- The young Men's Christian Association (YMCA) Was founded in London by George Williams.

June 6, 1882
- An electric Iron was patented by Henry W. Seely in NYC.

June 6, 1939
- Marian Wright Edelman, first African-American woman to be admitted to the Mississippi Bar, was born. She was the founder of the Children's Defense fund.

June 7, 1776
- Richard Henry Lee presents the "Lee Resolution" to the Continental Congress. The motion is seconded by John Adams and leads to the United States Declaration of Independence.

June 7, 1893
- Gandhi's first act of civil disobedience. Gandhi first Employed non-violent civil disobedience.

June 7, 1929
- Vatican City becomes a sovereign independent State. Vatican City is approx 110 acres with a population of Around 800.

June 7, 1948
- Edvard Benes resigns as President of Czechoslovakia rather than signing a Constitution making his nation a Communist state.

June 8, 1824
- Washing machine patented by Noah Cushing of Quebec

June 8, 1953
- The Supreme Court ruled that restaurants and bars in Washington D.C. are required to serve African-American customers.

June 8, 1968
- James Earl Ray, alleged assassin of Martin Luther King, Jr., captured.

June 8, 1998
- Kurt Waldheim, former Secretary-General of the United Nations, is elected president of Austria.

June 8, 1986
- Kurt Waldheim, former Sercretary-General of the
United Nations, is elected president of Austria.

June 8, 1998
- Head of State, General Sani Abacha dies of heart
attack and is buried in Kano.

June 8, 1999
- Nigeria Labour Congress (NLC) elects Mr. Adams
Oshiomole as the President of the Labour Congress.

June 9, 1870
- Charles Dickens, English writer (Authored David Copperfield), dies at 58.

June 9, 1898
- The British signed a 99-year lease for Hong Kong, located on the southeasterm coast of Chin. It was administered as a British Crown Colony until July 1, 1997, when its sovereignty reverted to the People's Republic of China.

DAYS OF HISTORY

June 9, 1944
- The Republic of Iceland was established.

June 9, 1946
- King Bhumibol Adulyadej ascends to the throne of Thailand. He is currently the world's longest reigning monarch.

June 9, 1978
- After 148 years, the leaders of the Church of Jesus Christ of Latter-Day Saints finally allowed black men to become priests.

June 10, 1793
- The Jardin des Plantes museum opens in Paris. A year later, it becomes the first public zoo.

June 10, 1973
- Washington replaced Philadelphia as U.S. capital.

June 10, 1915
- Girl Scouts founded.

June 10, 1942
- The entire male population of the Czech village of Lidice was massacred in retaliation for the death of Naze official Reinhard Heydrich.

June 10, 1967
- Israel, Syria, Jordan, Iraq and Egypt end "6-Day War" with United Nations help.

June 10, 1991
- Justice Andrew Otutu Obaseki bowed out of the Supreme Court with a call on his colleagues and the nation to strengthen the court's position as the
pride of Nigeria.

June 11, 1935
- Inventor Edwin Armstrong gives the first public demonstration of FM broadcasting in the United States, at Alpine, New Jersey.

June 11, 1935
- Inventor Edwin Armstrong gives the first public demonstration of FM broadcasting in the United States, at Alpine, New Jersey.

June 11, 1962
- Frank Morris, John Anglin and Clarence Anglin become the only prisoners to escape from the prison on Alcatraz Island.

June 11, 1963
- Alabama Governor George Wallace trying to ensure continued segregation is forced to end his blockade of the University of Alabama in Tuscaloosa and allows two African American students to enroll.

June 11, 1975
- British author and lecturer Denis Hill is found guilty a Ugandan tribunal of treason for criticizing Idi Amin.

June 11, 1979
- Film star John Wayne, also known as the "Duke," died of cancer.

June 12, 1898
- The Philippines declared their independence from Spain
Under rebel leader, Emilio Aguinaldo. The islands were named after King Philip II. Once freed from Spain, the island were then invaded and occupied by U.S. forces. They became an American colony and remained so until after World War II.

June 12, 1926
- Brazil quit the League of Nations in protest over plans to admit Germany.

June 12, 1965
- Big Bang theory of creation of universe was supported by announcement of discovery of new celestial bodies known as blue galaxies.

DAYS OF HISTORY

June 12, 1975
- In India the High Court of Allahabad declared Indira Gandhi's election invalid on grounds of alleged malpractices in an election petition filed by Raj Narain, who had repeatedly contested her parliamentary constituency of Rae Bareli without success.

June 12, 1991
- Russians went to the polls and elected Boris Yeltsin as President.

June 12, 1993
- In Nigeria, Chief Moshood Abiola was elected to the presidency in an election believed to be the freest and fairest in the country. But Gen. Ibrahim Babangida annulled the election.

June 13, 1415
- Henry the Navigator, the prince of Portugal, embarked on an expedition to Africa. This marked the beginning of Portuguese dominance of West Africa.

June 13, 1525
- Martin Luther marries Katharina von Bora, against the the celibacy rule decreed by the Roman Catholic Church for priests and nuns.

June 13, 1774
- Rhode Island becomes the first of Britain's North American colonies to ban the importation of slaves.

June 13, 1825
- Walter Hunt patents safety pin

June 13, 1966
- The Supreme Court issued its landmark Miranda vs. Arizona decision, ruling that criminal suspects must be informed of their constitutional rights prior to questioning by police.

June 13, 1967
- U.S. President Lyndon B. Johnson nominates Solicitor General Thurgood Marshall to become the first black justice on the U.S. Supreme Court.

June 14, 1642
- Massachusetts passed the first compulsory education law in the colonies.

June 14, 1777
- The Continental Congress in Philadelphia adopted the Stars and Stripes, created by Betsy Ross, as the national flag. America's Flag Day, commemorates the date when John Adams spoke the following words before the Continental Congress in Philadelphia. "Resolved, that the Union be thirteen stars, white on a blue field, representing a new constellation."

June 14, 1841
- The first Canadian parliament opened in Kingston.

June 14, 1520
- Pope Leo the Tenth threatened to excommunicate Martin Luther if he did not recant his religious beliefs.

June 14, 1752
- Benjamin Franklin and his son tested the relationship between electricity and lightning by flying a kite in a thunder storm.

June 15, 1846
- The United States and Britain signed a treaty settlinga boundary dispute between Canada and the United States in the Pacific Northwest at the 49th parallel. Great Britain and the U.S. agreed on a joint occupation of Oregon Territory.

June 15, 1947
- The All-Indian Congress accepted a British plan for the partition of India. Britain partitioned the subcontinent and Pakistan was founded as an independent country.

DAYS OF HISTORY

June 16, 1779
- Spain, in support of the US, declared war on England.

June 16, 1858
- In a speech accepting the Republican nomination for U.S. Senate candidate Abraham Lincoln said the slavery issue had to be resolved, declaring, "A house divided against itself cannot stand."

June 16, 1896
- Jean Peugeot, French auto manufacturer, was born.

June 16, 1903
- Ford Motor Co. was incorporated.

June 16, 1910
- The first Father's Day was celebrated in Spokane Washington by Mrs. John Bruce Dodd.

June 16, 1917
- The 1st Congress of Soviets convened in Russia.

June 17, 1703
- John Wesley, English evangelist and theologian, Was born. He founded the Methodist movement.

June 17, 1861
- President Abraham Lincoln witnessed Dr. Thaddeus Lowe demonstrate the use of a hot-air balloon.

June 17, 1885
- The Statue of Liberty arrives in New York Harbor.

June 17, 1944
- Iceland declared full independence from Denmark and became a republic.

June 17, 1950
- Surgeon Richard Lawler performed the first kidney
Transplant operation in Chicago.

June 17, 1972
- President Nixon's eventual downfall began when five men were arrested for breaking into the Democratic National Committee offices at the Watergate hotel.

June 18, 1812
- The War of 1812 began as the United States declared war against Great Britain and Ireland. In 2004 Walter R. Borneman authored "1812: The War That Forged a Nation."

June 18, 1948
- The United Nations Commission on Human Rights adopted its Universal Declaration of Human Rights.

June 18, 1995
- A private plane carrying the Angolan soccer team Crashed in Luanda, Angola, killing 48 people.

June 18, 1998
- In Nigeria six more political detainees were released following the death of the military dictator Gen Sanni Abacha.

June 18, 1942
- The U.S. Navy commissioned its first black officer, Harvard University medical student Bernard Whitfield Robinson.

June 19, 1829
Slavery was outlawed in U.S. territories. President Abraham Lincoln outlined his Emancipation Proclamation. News of the document reached the south and Texas through General Gordon Granger.

June 19, 1953
- Julius and Ethel Rosenberg were executed by electrocution at Sing Sing Prison in New York. They had been found guilty of providing vital information on the atomic bomb to the Soviet Union during 1944-45. They were the first U.S. civilians to be sentenced to death for espionage and were also the only married couple ever executed together in the U.S.

DAYS OF HISTORY

June 19, 1961
- Kuwait regained complete independence from Britain along with Qatar and Bahrain.

June 19, 1979
- In Mali, presidential and general elections were held. Moussa Traore was elected President and Mady Sangare was elected as Speaker of the National Assembly.

Birthday Baseball great Lou Gehrig (1903-1941),was born in New York City. He played in 2,130 consecutive games and seven World Series for the New York Yankees and had a lifetime batting average of 340. He contracted the degenerative muscle disease amyotrophic lateral sclerosis, now called 'Lou Gehrig's disease,' and died on June 2, 1941.

June 20, 1837
Princess Victoria became Queen Victoria of England on this day, following the death of her uncle, King William IV. The Princess was only 18 when she was called to rule Britannia.

June 20, 1840
- Samuel Morse receives the patent for the telegraph.

June 20, 1877
- Alexander Graham Bell installs the world's first commercial telephone service in Hamilton, Ontario, Canada.

June 20, 1944
- Nazis began mass extermination of Jews at Auschwitz.

June 20, 1960
- Independence of Mali and Senegal.

June 20, 1967
- Muhammad Ali was convicted of violating Selective Service laws by refusing to be drafted.

June 20, 1975
- The summer blockbuster movie "Jaws" is released about a great white shark attacking swimmers at Amity Island, a fictional summer resort town.

June 21, 1898
- The United States captures Guam from Spain.

June 21, 1915
- The U.S. Supreme Court hands down its decision in Guinn v. United States 238 US 347 1915, striking down an Oklahoma law denying the right to vote to some citizens.

June 21, 1919
- The Royal Canadian Mounted Police fire a volley into a crowd of unemployed war veterans, killing two, during the Winnipeg General Strike.

June 21, 1940
- The first successful west-to-east navigation of Northwest Passage begins at Vancouver, British Columbia.

June 22, 1989
- The government of Angola and the anti-Communist rebels of the UNITA movement agreed to a formal truce in their 14-year-old civil war.

June 22, 1990
- African National Congress leader Nelson Mandela addressed delegates at the United Nations, where he said victory for a democratic, non-racial South Africa was "within our grasp."

June 22, 1995
- Nigeria's former military ruler Gen. Olusegun Obasanjo and his chief deputy were charged with conspiracy to overthrow Gen. Sani Abacha's military government.

DAYS OF HISTORY

June 22, 1772
- Slavery was in effect outlawed in England by Chief Justice William Murray, First Eart of Mansfield, following the trial of James Somersett.

June 22, 1910
- German bacteriologist Paul Ehrlich announced a definitive Cure for syphilis.

June 23, 1848
- Antoine Joseph Sax patents the saxophone.

June 23, 1868
- Christopher Latham Sholes receives a patent for the typewriter.

June 23, 1894
The International Olympic Committee is founded at the Sorbonne, Paris, at the initiative of Baron Pierre de Coubertin.

June 23, 1981
- Alhaji Balarabe Musa is impeached by NPN-impeached dominated Kaduna State House of Assembly, making him
the first Nigerian state governor ever to be impeached.

June 23, 1993
- Nigeria's military dictator, Gen. Ibrahim Babangida, Voids results of presidential elections and halts return to democracy.

June 24, 1497
- Italian explorer John Cabot (1450 1498?), (aka Giovanni Caboto), on a voyage for England, landed in North America on what is now Newfoundland or the northem Cape Breton Island in Canada. He claimed the new land for King Henry VII.

June 24, 1793
- The first republican constitution in France was adopted.

June 24, 1930
- The 1st radar detection of planes was made at Anacostia, DC.

June 24, 1932
- A coup ended the absolute monarchy in Thailand.

June 24, 1942
- The German Africa Corps occupied Egypt.

June 24, 1950
- In Brazil the Maracana stadium in Rio was officially inaugurated for the opening of soccer's World Cup, the first in 12years due to WW II.

June 25, 1630
- The fork was introduced to American dining by Gov. Winthrop.

June 25, 1867
- The 1st barbed wire was patented by Lucien B. Smith of Ohio.

June 25, 1951
- The first Commercial color telecast took place as CBS transmitted a one-hour special from New York to our other cities.

June 25, 1975
- Mozambique became an independent state (twice the size of California), ending nearly five centuries of Portuguese rule.

June 25, 1991
- Slovenia proclaimed independence from Yugoslavia.

June 25, 1999
- In Nigeria representatives of the Ijaw, Itsekiri and Urhobo ethnic groups agreed to end ethnic strife and pursue a lasting peace through dialogue.

DAYS OF HISTORY

June 26, 1498
- Toothbrush was invented, In China the first toothbrushes with hog bristles began to show up. Hog bristle brushes remained the best until the invention of nylon.

June 26, 1819
The bicycle was patented by W.K. Clarkson Jr. of New York City.

June 26, 1860
- The first railway line in South Africa between Durban and the Point, was officially opened.

June 26, 1979
- Heavyweight boxing champion, Muhammd Ali, Confirmed to reporters that he'd sent a letter to the World Boxing Association resigning his title, saying his third announced retirement was indeed final.

June 26, 1990
- African National Congress leader, Nelson Mandela,
Nelson Mandela, addressed the U.S. Congress, asking for "material resources" to hasten the end of white-led rule.

June 26, 1945
- The United Nations Organisation Charter was signed in San Francisco by 50 nations. The Charter was ratified on October 24, 1945.

Birthday
American author, Pearl Buck (1892-1973), was born in Hillsboro, West Virginia. She became a noted authority on China and wrote books including the Good Earth which revealed the mysterious Chinese Culture to Western readers, She received a Nobel Prize in 1938 for her many books.

June 27, 1844
- Joseph Smith, Jr., founder of the Church of Jesus Christ of Latter-day Saints, and his brother Hyrum Smith, are murdered by a mob at the Carthage, Illinois jail.

June 27, 1890
- George Dixon becomes first black boxing champ (Bantam weight)

June 27, 1923
- Capt. Lowell H. Smith and Lt. John P. Richter perform the first ever aerial refueling in a DH-4B biplane.

June 27, 1941
- Romanian governmental forces, allies of Nazi Germany, launch one of the most violent pogroms in Jewish history in the city of Iai, (Romania), resulting in the murder of at least 13,266 Jews.

June 27, 1954
- The world's first nuclear power station opens in Obninsk, near Moscow.

June 27, 1967
- The world's first ATM is installed in Enfield, Lodon.

June 28, 1389
- Ottomans defeat Serbian army in the bloody Battle of Kosovo, opening the way for the Ottoman conquest of Southeastern Europe (see Vidovdan).

June 28, 1776
- American Revolutionary War: Thomas Hickey, Continental Army private and bodyguard to General George Washington, is hanged for mutiny and sedition.

June 28, 1807
- Second British invasion of the Rio de la Plata; John Whitelock lands at Ensenada on an attempt to recapture Buenos Aires and is defeated by the fierce resistance of the locals.

DAYS OF HISTORY

June 28, 1841
- The Theater de l'Academie Royale de Musique in Paris premieres the ballet Giselle.

June 29, 1860
- The last stone was laid at Minot's Ledge (Massachusetts) Lighthouse. The stone tower replaced an iron-pile Lighthouse that had been destroyed by a storm in April 1851

June 29, 1897
- The Chicago Clubs scored 36 runs in a ball game against Louisville, setting a record for runs scored by a team in single game.

June 29, 1901
- The first edition of "Editor & Publisher" was issued. It was a newspaper for the newspaper industry.

June 29, 1925
- A patent for the frosted electric light bulb was filed by Marvin pipkin. The frosting inside the light bulb created less glare because it diffused the light emitted,
spreading it over a wider area, providing a much softer glow.

June 29, 1932
- The second daytime serial to be heard on network radio was "Vic and Sade" which debutd on the NBC Blue radio
network this day. Radio's first daytime drama was "Clara Lu and Em", which premiered on NBC in 1931.

June 30, 1997
- In Hong Kong, the Union Jack was lowered for the last time over Government House as Britain
prepared to hand the colony back to China after ruling it for 156 years.

June 30, 1999
- In Nigeria, Federal Government scraps PTF and appoints Dr. Haroun Adamu as Sole Administrator to oversee its winding up.

June 30, 1893
- Excelsior diamond (blue-white 995 carats) was discovered.

June 30, 1894
- Korea declared independence from China and asked for Japanese aid.

June 30, 1896
W.S. Hadaway patented an electric stove.

June 30, 1934
- The Night of the Long Knives, Adolf Hitler's violent purge of his political rivals in Germany, takes place.

June 30, 1960
- Independence was granted to the Congo by Belgium.

July 1, 1910
- The original Comiskey Park (Pictured 1990), home of the Chicago White Sox for eight decades, held its opening day under the name White Sox Park.
(The home team lost to the St. Louis Browns, 2-0.)

July 1, 1946
- The United States exploded a 20-kiloton atomic bomb near Bikini Atoll in the Pacific

July 1, 1980
- President Jimmy Carter signed the Motor Carrier Act which considerably deregulated the U.S. trucking industry.

July 1, 1980
- "O Canada" was proclaimed the national anthem of Canada..

DAYS OF HISTORY

July 1, 2000
- The Confederate flag was removed from atop South Carolina's Statehouse.

July 3, 1608
- The city of Quebec was founded as a trading post by Samuel de Champlain. The French adventurer, Etienne Brule, accompanied Champlain to North America and was reportedly eaten by the Huron Indians.

July 3, 1950
- American and North Korean forces clashed for the first time in the Korean War. U.S. carrier-based planes attacked airfields in the Pynogyang-Chinnampo area of North Korea in the first air-strike of the Korean War.

July 3, 1962
- French President, Charles de Gaulle, pronounced Algeria an independent country following the July 1 elections. De Gaulle evacuated Algeria and a million settlers flooded into France.

July 3, 1976
- The raid on Entebe Airport in Uganda occurred as an Israeli commando unit rescued 103 hostages on a hijacked Air France airliner. The jet had been en route from Tel Aviv to Paris when it was hijacked by pro-Palestinian guerrillas.
Three hostages, seven hijackers and 20 Ugandan soldiers were killed during the rescue.

July 3, 1988
Flight 655 was destroyed while flying over the Persian Gulf after the U.S. Navy Warship, Vincennes, fired two surface-to-air missiles, killing all 290 passengers aboard. A subsequent U.S. military inquiry cited stress related human failure for the mistaken identification of the civilian airbus as an enemy F-14 fighter jet.

July 4, 1636
- City of Providence, Rhode Island, was formed.

July 4, 1712
- Twelve slaves were executed for starting a slave uprising in New York that killed nine whites.

July 4, 1776
- The Continental Congress approved adoption of the amended Declaration of Independence, prepared by Thomas Jefferson and signed by John Hancock- President of the Continental Congress and Charles Thomson, Congress secretary, without dissent.

July 4, 1785
- The first Fourth of July parade was held in Bristol, Rhode Island. It served as a prayerful walk to celebrate independence from England.

July 4, 1802
- The United State Military Academy opened its Doors at West Point, New York, welcoming the first 10 cadets.

July 5, 1776
- The Declaration of Independence was first printed by John Dunlop in Philadelphia.

July 5, 1811
- Venezuela became the first South American country to declare independence from Spain.

July 5, 1942
- Ian Fleming graduated from a training school For spies in Canada.

July 5, 1945
- Labour Party won British parliamentary election.

DAYS OF HISTORY

July 1, 2000
- The Confederate flag was removed from atop South Carolina's Statehouse.

July 3, 1608
- The city of Quebec was founded as a trading post by Samuel de Champlain. The French adventurer, Etienne Brule, accompanied Champlain to North America and was reportedly eaten by the Huron Indians.

July 3, 1950
- American and North Korean forces clashed for the first time in the Korean War. U.S. carrier-based planes attacked airfields in the Pynogyang-Chinnampo area of North Korea in the first air-strike of the Korean War.

July 3, 1962
- French President, Charles de Gaulle, pronounced Algeria an independent country following the July 1 elections. De Gaulle evacuated Algeria and a million settlers flooded into France.

July 3, 1976
- The raid on Entebe Airport in Uganda occurred as an Israeli commando unit rescued 103 hostages on a hijacked Air France airliner.The jet had been en route from Tel Aviv to Paris when it was hijacked by pro-Palestinian guerrillas.
Three hostages, seven hijackers and 20 Ugandan soldiers were killed during the rescue.

July 3, 1988
Flight 655 was destroyed while flying over the Persian Gulf after the U.S. Navy Warship, Vincennes, fired two surface-to-air missiles, killing all 290 passengers aboard. A subsequent U.S. military inquiry cited stress related human failure for the mistaken identification of the civilian airbus as an enemy F-14 fighter jet.

July 4, 1636
- City of Providence, Rhode Island, was formed.

July 4, 1712
- Twelve slaves were executed for starting a slave uprising in New York that killed nine whites.

July 4, 1776
- The Continental Congress approved adoption of the amended Declaration of Independence, prepared by Thomas Jefferson and signed by John Hancock-President of the Continental Congress and Charles Thomson, Congress secretary, without dissent.

July 4, 1785
- The first Fourth of July parade was held in Bristol, Rhode Island. It served as a prayerful walk to celebrate independence from England.

July 4, 1802
- The United State Military Academy opened its Doors at West Point, New York, welcoming the first 10 cadets.

July 5, 1776
- The Declaration of Independence was first printed by John Dunlop in Philadelphia.

July 5, 1811
- Venezuela became the first South American country to declare independence from Spain.

July 5, 1942
- Ian Fleming graduated from a training school For spies in Canada.

July 5, 1945
- Labour Party won British parliamentary election.

DAYS OF HISTORY

July 5, 1991
- Celebrated television actress, Chief (Mrs,) Elsie Olusola, who played 'sisi clara' in the longest running NTA Soap Opera "Village Headmaster" died.

July 6, 1785
- The dollar is unanimously chosen as the monetary unit for the United States.

July 6, 1885
- Louis Pasteur successfully tests his vaccine against rabies. The patient is Joseph Meister, a boy who was bitten by a rabid dog.

July 6, 1858
- The shoe manufacturing machine was patented by Lyman Blake of Abington, MA.

July 6, 1957
- Althea Gibson won the Wimbledon women's singles tennis title. She was the first black person to win the event.

July 6, 1966
- Malawi becomes a republic, with Hastings Banda as the first President.

July 6, 1991
- Nigeria's football ambassador, Mudasiru Babatunde Lawal collapsed and died at his Ibadan residence.

July 7, 1753
- British Museum founded by an Act of Parliament (Opens in 1759)

July 7, 1865
- American Civil War: four conspirators in the assassination of President Abraham Lincoln are hanged.

July 7, 1928
- Sliced bread is sold for the first time by the Chillicothe Baking Company of Chillicothe, Missouri.

July 7, 1981
- Arizona Judge Sandra Day O' Connor is nominated by President Ronald Reagan to become the first female justice on the U.S. Supreme Court.

July 7, 1998
- Chief M.K.O. Abiola, acclaimed winner of the June 12, 1993 presidential election, dies of cardiac arrest while having a meeting with Nigeria and United States officials in Abuja.

July 8, 1990
- West Germany won the World Cup soccer championship by defeating Argentina, 1-to-0.

July 8, 1996
- In Niger the military ruler suspended the Independent National electoral commission after early results showed him losing.

July 8, 1998
- In Afghanistan the Taliban decreed that television was corrupting Afghan society and issued an edict that banned televisions, videocassette recorders, videos and satellite dishes.

July 8, 1999
- In southern Nigeria activists claimed to have Capture and shut down 61 oil wells operated by Shell workers were also ejected from wells in the region of Egbama East and Egbema West.

July 8, 1755
- Britain broke off diplcmatic relations with France as their disputes in the New World intensified.

July 9, 1816
- Argentina declared independence from Spain.

DAYS OF HISTORY

July 9, 1900
- Queen Victoria signed The Commonwealth of Australia Constitution Act, uniting 6 separate colonies under a federal government, effective Jan 1, 1901.

July 9, 1972
- The body Kwame Nkrumah (1909-1972), former head of Ghana (1915-1966), was returned to Nkroful, Ghana, for burial.

July 9, 1996
- In Rwanda the Tutsi dominated army carried out an Operation against Hutu insurgents in Karago and Giciye Villages and 62 people were killed. The area was the home of the Hutu president Juvenal Habyarimana.

Aug. 9, 1997
- In Kenya armed police shut down the University of Nairobi and clubbed students who demanded free and fair elections.

July 10, 1943
- The Allied invasion of Italy began with an attack on the island of Sicily. The British entry into Syracuse was the first Allied success in Europe. General Dwight D. Eisenhower Labeled the invasion "the first page in the liberation of the European Continent."

July 10, 1971
- In Morocco a coup against King Hassan at the Skhirat Palace faied. Nearly 100 guests were killed. The coup leaders were executed three days later.

July 10, 1973
- The Bahamas gained their independence after 250 years as a British Crown Colony.

July 10, 1991
- Boris Yeltsin took the oath of office, becoming the first popularly elected President in Russia's thousand-year history.

Birthday- Theologian and founder of Presbyterianism, John Calvin (1509-1564), was born in Noyon, France.

Birthday- Tennis player, Arthur Ashe (1943-1993), was born in Richmond, Virginia. He won a total of 33 titles including the U.S. men's singles championship and U.S. Open in 1968 and the men's singles at Wimbledon in 1975.

In 1992, he announced he had likely contracted HIV through a transfusion during heart surgery and began a $5m fund raising effort on behalf of Arthur Ashe Foundation for the Defeat of AIDS. He died from pneumonia in New York, February 6, 1993.

July 11, 1804
- Former vice president of the United States Aaron Burr fatally wounded former secretary of the treasury Alexander Hamilton died the following afternoon.

July 11, 1859
A Tale of Two Cities by Charles Dickens is Published.

July 11, 1895
- First motion picture is shown in Paris by the Lumiere brothers.

July 11, 1897
- Salomon August Andree leaves Spitsbergen to attempt to reach the North pole by ballon. He later crashes and dies.

July 11, 1960
- Ivory Coast, Dahomey, Upper Volta and Niger declare independence.

July 11, 1977
- The Rev. Dr. Martin Luther King, Jr., Was posthumously Medal of Freedom for his work to advance civil rights.

DAYS OF HISTORY

July 11, 1991
- All 265 people on a chartered Canadian DC-8 air craft carrying Moslem pilgrims home to Nigeria, died when it crashed and burst into flames in Saudi Arabia.

July 12, 1996
- A divorce settlement between Lady Diana Spencer and Charles, the Prince of Wales was Agreed upon. Diana would be called "Her Royal Highness" and would receive about $22.5 mill plus an annual $600.000 to maintain her private office.

July 12, 1998
- In France the French team beat Brazil, 3-0, for its first World Cup soccer championship.

July 12, 2004
- Newspapers in Senegal and the Central African Republic suspended publication to protest the jailings of leading journalists.

July 12, 2006
- In Nigeria 2 explosions hit oil installations belonging to an Italian oil company along two Agip pipelines in Bayelsa state.

July 14, 1933
- Gleichschaltung: In Germany, all political parties are outlawed except the Nazi Party.

July 14, 1949
- U.S.S.R. explodes that 1st atom bomb.

July 14, 1941
- 6,000 Lithuanian Jews are exterminated at Viszalsyan Camp.

July 14, 1933
- Germany began mandatory sterilization of those with hereditary illness.

July 14, 1958
- Iraqi Revolution: In Iraq the monarchy is overthrown by Arab nationalists and Abdul Karim Kassem becomes the nation's new leader.

July 14, 1969
- The United States $500, $1,000, $5,000 and $10.000 Bills are officially withdrawn from circulation.

July 15, 1795
- The 'Marseillaise' is adopted as the French national anthem.

July 15, 1869
- Margarine was patented in France by Hippolyte Mege Mouries.

July 15, 1870
- Georgia became the last of the Confederate States to be readmitted to the Union.

July 15, 1916
- William Boeing incorporated Pacific Aero Products, Later named the Boeing Co.

July 15, 1940
- The world's tallest man (8 feet, 11.1 inches), Robert Wadlow, died.

July 15, 1975
- The Russian Soyuz and the U.S. Apollo launched. The Apollo-Soyuz mission was the first international manned spaceflight.

July 16, 1622
- The beginning of the Islamic calendar. During this year the prophet Mohammad left Mecca and went to Medina.

July 16, 1661
- The first banknotes in Europe are issued by the Swedish bank Stockholms Banco.

July 16, 1790
- The District of Columbia was established as the seat of the United States government.

July 16, 1880
- Emily Stowe becomes the first female physician licensed to practice medicine in Canada.

DAYS OF HISTORY

July 16, 1935
- The world's first parking meter is installed in the Oklahoma capital, Oklahoma City.

July 16, 1945
- The first atomic bomb was tested in Alamogordo, N.M.

July 16, 1950
- The largest crowd in sporting history- 199,854-watched the World Cup soccer finals in Rio de Janeiro, Brazil.

July 17, 1799
- Napoleon Bonaparte of France incorporated Italy into his empire.

July 17, 1967
- China detonated its 1st hydrogen bomb and became the World's 4th thermonuclear power.

July 17, 1977
- The Olubadan of Ibadan, Oba Gbadamosi Adebimpe, Died aged 84 years, succeeded by Chief Daniel Tayo Akinbiyi, the Otun Olubadan of Ibadan.

July 17, 1998
- A diplomatic conference adopts the Rome Statute of the International Criminal Court, establishing a permanent international court to prosecute individuals for genocide, crime against humanity, war crimes, and the crime of aggression.

July 17, 1918
- In the Russian town of Ekaterinburg in Siberia, former Czar, Nicholas II; his wife Alexandra, and their five children were brutally murdered by Bolsheviks.

July 17, 1996
TWA Flight 800 departed Kennedy International Airport in New York bound for Paris, but exploded in mid-air 12 minutes after takeoff, apparently the result of a mechanical failure. The Beoing 747 jet crashed into Atlantic Ocean off the Coast of Long Island about 8:45p.m. All 212 passengers and 17 crew members on board were killed.

Birthday Puerto Rican patriot, Luis Munoz-Rivera (1859-1916), was born in Barranquitas, Puerto Rico. He worded tirelessly to attain self-government for his Homeland.

July 18, 1536
- Pope's authority declared void in England

July 18, 1872
- Britain introduces secret ballot voting.

July 18, 1898
- Marie and Pierre Curie announce the discovery of a new element and proposed to call it polonium.

July 18, 1918
_ Birth of South African statesman and anti-Apartheid leader Nelson Rolihlahla Mandela at Mvezo, Umtata District, Transkei, South Africa.

July 18, 1925
- Nazi leader Adolf Hitler publishers the first volume his Personal manifesto, Mein Kampf which was a bitter and turgid narrative filled with anti-Semitic outpourings, disdain for morality, worship of power, and the blueprints for his plan of Nazi world domination.

July 18, 1963
- The final result on creation of Mid-Western Region of Nigeria was published. Votes already counted showed an average of 75.6% in favour of the new region.

DAYS OF HISTORY

July 19, 1988
- Jesse Jackson brought his 1988 presidential campaign to an emotionally charged close at the Democratic National Convention in Atlanta, telling party faithful to unite because "the only time we win is when we come together."

July 19, 2002
- In Abiteye, Nigeria, unarmed women occupying at least four Chevron Texaco facilities took two hostages in a bid to meet with oil executives.

July 19, 1814
- Samuel Colt, inventor of the first practical revolver, was born.

July 19, 1848
- The first women's rights convention convened in Seneca Falls, New York.

July 20, 1810
- Colombia declared independence from Spain.

July 20, 1868
- The 1st use of tax stamps on cigarettes.

July 20, 1872
- Mahlon Loomis patented a wireless radio.

July 20, 1944
- President Roosevelt was nominated for an unprecedented fourth term of office at the Democratic National Convention in Chicago.

July 20, 1949
- Israel's 19 month war of independence ended with a ceasefire agreement with Syria.

July 20, 1951
- Jordan's King Abdullah Ibn Hussein was assassinated in Jerusalem by a Palestinian extremist. Prince Hussein (15) witnessed the murder.

July 21, 1831
- Belgium became independent as Leopold was proclaimed King of the Belgians.

July 21, 1960
- Sirimavo Bandaranaike became the first woman Prime minister of Ceylon twice 1960-65 and 1970-77. Under her leadership a republican constitution was adopted in 1972 and the name of Ceylon changed to Sri Lanka.

July 21, 1983
- The coldest temperature ever measured on Earth was -129 Fahrenheit (-89 Celsius) at the Russian Vostok Station in Antarctica.

July 21, 1994
- Britain's Labor Party elected Tony Blair its new leader, succeeding the late John Smith.

July 21, 2003
- In southwest Cameroon water-logged hillsides gave way after a week of heavy rain, killing at least 21 people.

July 22, 1933
- Wiley Post becomes first person to fly solo around the world traveling 15,596 miles in 7 days, 18 hours and 45 minutes.

July 22, 1944
- The Polish Committee of National Liberation publishes its manifesto, starting the period of Communist rule in Poland.

July 22, 1999
- The Speaker of the House of Representative, Alhaji Salisu Buhari resigns after confessing to certificate forgery and age falsification.

July 22, 2003
- Former Iraqi dictator Saddam Hussein's sons, Qusay and Uday Hussein, are killed after a three-hour firefight with U.S. forces in the northern Iraqi city of Mosul.

DAYS OF HISTORY

July 23, 1829
- In the United States, William Austin Burt patents the Typographer, a precursor to the typewriter.

July 23, 1840
- The Province of Canada is created by the Act of Union.

July 23, 1881
- The Federation Internationale de Gymnastique, the world's oldest international sport federation, is founded.

July 23, 1920
- British East Africa renamed Kenya and becomes a British crown colony.

July 23, 1984
- Vanessa Williams becomes the first Miss America to resign when she surrenders her crown after nude photos of her appeared in Penthouse magazine.

July 23, 1999
- Crown Prince Mohammed Ben Al-Hassan is crowned King Mohammed VI of Morocco on the death of his father.

July 24, 1883
- Matthew Webb (b.1848). the first person to swin in the English Channel (1875), drowned while trying to swin across the Niagara River just below the falls.

July 24, 1922
_ League of Nations gave Egyptian mandate to Britain. Egypt remained a British Protectorate until the Anglo-Egyptian treaty was signed on August 26, 1936.

July 24, 1943
- During World War II in Europe. The Royal Air Force Conducted Operation Gomorrah, raiding Hamburg, while tossing bales of aluminum foil strips overboard to cause German radar screens to see a blizzard of false echoes.
As a result, only 12 of 791 Allied bombers involved were shot down.

July 24, 1945
- At the conclusion of the Potsdam Conference in Germany, Winston Churchill, Harry Truman and China's representatives issued a demand for unconditional Japanese surrender. The Japanese, unaware the demand was backed up by an Atomic bomb, rejected the Potsdam Declaration on July 26.

July 24, 1990
- Reports of mass Iraqi troops on the Kuwait border raised Concerns that Iraq was planning to invade the country which is one of the richest oil nations in the world. Just over one weeklater on August 2, 1990 Iraq did invade Kuwait and within two days most of the Kuwaiti Armed Forces and Iraq was in control.

Birthday American pilot, Amelia Earhart (1898-1937), was born in Atchison, Kansas. She became the first woman to fly solo across the Atlantic and to fly solo from Hawaii to California. She perished during a flight from New Guinea to Howland Island over the Pacific Ocean on July 3, 1937.

July 25, 1837
- The first commercial use of an electric telegraph is successfully demonstrated by William Cooke and Charles Wheatstone on 25 July 1837 between
Euston and Camden Town in London.

July 25, 1866
- The U.S. Congress passes legislation authorizing the rank of General of the Army (commonly called "5-star general"). Lieutenant General Ulysses S. Grant becomes the first to be promoted to this rank.

July 25, 1908
_ Ajinomoto is founded. Kikunae Ikeda of the Tokyo Imperial University discovers that a key ingredient in Konbu soap stock is monosodium glutamate (MSG), and patents a process for manufacturing it.

DAYS OF HISTORY

July 25, 1943
- Benito Mussolini captured, dismissed as premier of Italy during WW II.

July 26, 1775
- The Continental Congress established a postal system for the colonies with Benjamin Franklin as the first postmaster general in Philadelphia.

July 26, 1847
- Liberia became the first African colony to became an independent state. A mutual agreement between the settlers and the American Colonization Society created the republic of Liberia. Joseph Jenkins Roberts, the Virginia-born son of free blacks, was elected the first president of Liberia.

July 26, 1942
- Roman Catholic churches protested the Dutch bishops' stand against the spread of Judaism.

July 26, 1944
- The first desegregation in the US Army.

July 27 1866
- Cyrus W. Field finished laying out the first successful underwater telegraph cable between North America and Europe.

July 27, 1962
- Martin Luther King Jr. was jailed in Albany, Georgia.

July 27, 1965
- 36th President of the United States, Lyndon Johnson signed a bill requiring cigarette makers to print health warnings on all cigarette packages about the effects of smoking.

July 27, 1996
- A bomb explosion rocks the Olympic Park in Atlanta City killing two persons and wounding 111 others.

July 27, 1998
- Monica Lewinsky was interviewed for five hours by Prosecutors in New York in a possible in New York in a possible prelude to an immunity deal.

July 28, 1868
- The 14th Amendment to the Constitution of the United States is passed, establishing African-American citizenship and guaranteeing due process of law.

July 28, 1945
- A. U. S. Army B-25 bomber crashes into the 79th floor of the Empire State Building killing 14 and injuring 26.

July 28, 1977
- The Federal Government gave new directives banning Civil servants form spending their vacation leave outside Nigeria or Africa except in deserving cases.

July 28, 1985
- President Apolo Milton Obote of Uganda is ousted in a military coup. Basilio Olara Okello takes power as the Chairman of the Military Council.

July 28, 2001
- Australian Ian Thorpe becomes the first swimmer to win six gold medals at a single World Championships.

July 29, 1833
- William Wilberforce (b. 1759), English abolitionist, died. He was a politician, philanthropist and was prominent from 1787 in the struggle to abolish the slave trade and slavery itself in British overseas possessions.

July 29, 1914
- Transcontinental telephone service began with the first phone conversation between New York and San Francisco.

DAYS OF HISTORY

July 29, 1921
- Adolf Hitler became the president of the Nationalist Socialist German Workers' Party (Nazis)

July 29, 1957
- The International Atomic Energy Agency is established.

July 29, 1981
- Charles, Prince of Wales and Lady Diana Spencer marry at St Paul's Cathedral, before 3,500 invited guests and an estimated worldwide television audience of 750 million People.

July, 30, 1792
- The French national anthem "La Marseillaise" by Claude Joseph Rouget de Lisle, was first sung on the
Streets by volunteers (federes) from Marseille upon their entry into Paris.

July 30, 1863
- Henry Ford (d. 1947), founder of the Ford Motor Company and developer of the Model T, was born in Dearborn Township, Mich.

July 30, 1935
- The 1st Penguin book was published in England and Started the paperback revolution. The sixpenny books
made a 1st blow to the library system.

July 30, 1947
- Arnold Schwarzenegger, an Austrian American Bodybuilder, actor, model, businessman, and politician, who is currently serving as the 38th Governor of California since 2003, was born in Thal Bei Graz, Austria.

July 30, 1956
- US motto "In God We Trust" was authorized.

July 31, 1498
- During his third voyage to the Western Hemisphere, Christopher Columbus arrived at an island he named Trinidad because of its three hills.

July 31, 1776
- During the American Revolution, Francis Salvador became the first Jew to die in the conflict. He had also been the first Jew elected to office in Colonial America, voted a member of the South Carolina Provincial Congress in January 1775.

July 31, 1960
Elijah Muhammad, an African American religious leader and activist called for a black state. He was the leader of the Nation of Islam organization from 1934 until his death. He was a mentor to Malcolm X, Louis Farrakhan, and boxer Cassius Marcellus Clay, Jr., whom he renamed Muhammad Ali. He was leader of Nation of Islam.

July 31, 1966
- Alabamans burnt Beatle products due to John Lennon's remark that the Beatles were more popular than Jesus Christ.

July 31, 1998
- In South Africa, the Truth and Reconciliation Commission closed down after two years of hearings. A report was released in October.

Aug. 1, 1291
- The Swiss Confederation is formed with the Signature of the Federal Charter.

Aug. 1, 1461
- Edward IV is crowned king of England.

Aug. 1, 1498
- Christopher Columbus becomes the first European to visit Venezuela.

DAYS OF HISTORY

Aug. 1, 1774
- Joseph Priestley isolates oxygen for the first time.

Aug. 1, 1793
- The metric unit of mass, the kilogram, is introduced in France

Aug. 1, 1834
- Slavery Abolition is abolished in the British Empire as the Slavery Abolition Act 1833 comes into force.

Aug. 1, 1873
- The first cable streetcar in America began operation on Clay Street Hill in San Francisco, CA.

Aug. 1, 1953
- The first aluminum-faced building constructed in America was completed.

Aug. 2, 1790
- The first US Census is conducted.

Aug. 2, 1798
- French Revolutionary Wars: Battle of the Nile (Battle of Aboukir Bay) concludes in a British victory.

Aug. 2, 1903
- Fall of the Ottoman Empire: Unsuccessful uprising led by the Internal Macedonian-Adrianople Revoloutionary Organization against Ottoman Turkey, also known as the Ilinden-Preobrazhenie Uprising.

Aug. 2, 1916
- World War I: Austrian sabotage causes the sinking of the Italian battleship Leonardo da Vinci in Taranto.

Aug. 3, 1911
- Airplanes were used for the first time in a military capacity when Italian planes reconnoitered Turkish lines near Tripoli.

Aug. 3, 1923
- Calvin Coolidge was sworn in as the 30th president of the United States, following the death of Warren G. Harding. Traditionally, the president is sworn in by the chief justice of the Supreme Court but at 2:30 a.m. on August 3, 1923, Coolidge's father, a notary public, administered the oath of office to his son by the light of a kerosene lamp.

Aug. 3, 1934
- Adolf Hitler becomes the supreme leader of Germany by joining the offices of President and Chancellor into fuhrer.

Aug. 3, 1960
- Niger gained independence from France. Hamani Diori was president.

Aug. 4, 1875
- The first Convention of Colored Newspapermen was held in Cincinnati, Ohio.

Aug. 4, 1958
- In Nigeria, Dr Kingsley Ozumba Mbadiwe announced the formation of a new party designated Democratic Party of Nigeria and the Cameroons advocating a Federal form of Government based on Socialist Ideology.

Aug. 4, 1961
- Barack Obama, later US Senator from Illinois, and 44th President of the United States, Nobel Peace Prize laureate, was born in Honolulu to a Black Kenyan father and a white American mother.

Aug. 4, 1962
- Nelson Mandela was captured by South African Police.

Aug. 4, 1984
- The African republic Upper Volta changes its name to Burkina Faso.

DAYS OF HISTORY

Aug. 5, 1735
- Freedom of the press: New York Weekly Journal Writer John Peter Zenger is acquitted of seditious libel against the royal governor of New York, on the basis that what he had published was true.

Aug. 5, 1891
- The 1st travelers checks were issued by American Express.

Aug. 5, 1974
- President Richard Nixon admitted that he ordered a cover-up of the Watergate break-in for political as well as national security reasons. One of the secret recordings, known as the "smoking gun" tape, was released.

Aug. 5, 1977
- In Nigeria, the Oyo State Government directed all pubic officers serving in the state to swear to an affidavit confirming that they had renounced membership of any secret cults they belonged to.

Aug. 6, 1945
- In 1945, the first atomic bomb used in World War II was dropped on Hiroshima, Japan. The weapon, code-named "Little Boy", was dropped from a United States Air Force B-29 bomber, The 393d Bombardment Squadron B-29 Enola Gay, piloted and commanded by 509th Composite Group commander Colonel Paul Tibbets.

Aug. 6, 1979
- The Mauritanian government has conceded defeat against the Polisario Front after three years of bitter
fighting for the southern section of Spanish Sahara (now Western Sahara), Rio de Oro. The country was divided between Mauritania and Morocco
when the Spanish pulled out in 1976.

Aug. 6, 1990
- The African National Congress in South Africa had announced its intention to halt guerrilla attacks as part of the on-going negotiations for the end of minority White rule.

Aug. 7, 1802
- Napoleon orders re-instatement of slavery on St Domingue (Haiti)

Aug. 7, 1888
- Theophilus Van Kannel of Phila patents revolving door.

Aug. 7, 1930
- Richard Bedford Bannet forms Canadian government.

Aug. 7, 1959
- The United States launched Explorer 6, which sent back a picture of Earth

Aug. 7, 1960
- Ivory Coast (C'te d'Ivoire) gains independence from France.

Aug. 7, 1987
- Lynne Cox becomes the first person to swim from the United States to the United States to the Soviet Union, making the 2.7 mile trip through the frigid Waters of the Bering Strait

Aug. 7, 1998
- The United States embassy bombings in Dar es Salaam, Tanzania and Nairobi, Kenya kill Approximately 212 people.

Aug. 8, 1786
- The US Congress adopted the silver dollar and Decimal system of money.

Aug. 8, 1815
- Napoleon Bonaparte set sail for St. Helena, in the South Atlantic, to spend the remainder of his days in exile.

DAYS OF HISTORY

Aug. 8, 1786
- The US Congress adopted the silver dollar and Decimal system of money.

Aug. 8, 1815
- Napoleon Bonaparte set sail for St. Helena, in the South Atlantic, to spend the remainder of his days in exile.

August 8, 1854
- Smith and Wesson patented metal bullet cartridges.

Aug. 8, 1899
- The first household refrigerating machine was patented.

Aug. 8, 1955
- Fidel Castro formed his "July 26th Movement."

Aug. 8, 1974
- President Nixon announced he would resign his office 12PM Aug. 9, following damaging revelations in the Watergate scandal.

Aug. 8, 1988
- U.N. Secretary-General Javier Perez de Cuellar Announced a cease-fire between Iran and Iraq. This became a Iraq national holiday until it was abolished in 2003.

Aug. 9, 1790
- The Columbia returned to Boston Harbor after a three-Year voyage, becoming the first ship to carry the American flag around the world.

Aug. 9, 1907
- The first Boy Scout encampment concludes at Brownsea Island in Southern England.

Aug. 9, 1942
- Mahatma Gandhi and 50 others were arrested in Bombay after the passing of a "quit India" campaign by the All-India Congress.

Aug. 9, 1963
- In Nigeria, the constitutional proposals were approved by the House of Representatives after an Opposition amendment calling for the retention of the Judicial Service Commission had been overwhelmingly defeated.

Aug. 10, 1869
- O.B. Brown of Malden, MA patented the motion-picture projector.

Aug. 10, 1885
- The nation's first electric streetcar railway opened in Baltimore.

Aug. 10, 1909
- A sizeable gold deposit was found in the Banket formation, Rhodesia, which extends for over six miles underground.

Aug. 10, 1948
- Candid Camera makes its television debut after being on Radio for a year as Candid Microphone.

Aug. 10, 1977
- The Assembly of the World Confederation of Organization of the Teaching Profession (WCOTP) ended its eight-day conference in Lagos.

August 10, 1985
- Madonna's album "Like a Virgin" became the first solo album by a female artist to be certified for sales of five million copies.

DAYS OF HISTORY

Aug. 11, 1836
- Cato Maximilian Guldberg a Norwegian chemist was born on 11 Aug. 1836 who, with his brother-in-law Peter Waage, formulated the law Peter mass action (1864), which details the effects of concentration, mass, and temperature on chemical reaction rates. The law states that A + B > >C the rate of reaction is proportional to [A][B], Where [A] and [B] are concentrations.

Aug. 11, 1940
- The British RAF raids airfields and Italian military bases, a week before Mussolini orders General Rodolfo Graziani to in invade Egypt from Libya. (World War II: North Africa).

Aug. 11, 1960
- Chad became independent from France, but remained within the French community. Francois Tombalbaye became the 1st present.

Aug. 12, 1865
- British surgeon Joseph Lister became the first doctor to use An antiseptic during surgery.

Aug. 12, 1887
- Thomas Edison makes the first sound recording.

Aug. 12, 1969
- Echo, the worlds first communication satellite, launched by the US.

Aug. 12, 1977
Oba Daniel Odetayo Akinbiyi was installed the 36th Olubadan at a ceremony in Ibadan in which the Oyo State governor, Brigadier David Jemibewon presented him the instrument of office.

August 12, 1990
- South Africa is barred from the Olympic Games in Tokyo as a sanction against its Apartheid policies.

Aug. 13, 1868
- A magnitude 9.0 quake in Africa, Peru (later Chile), Generated catastrophic tsunamis; more than 25,000 people were killed in South America.

Aug. 13, 1892
- The first issue of the "Afro American" newspaper was published in Baltimore, Maryland.

Aug. 13, 1926
- Fidel Castro, revolutionary leader, president, was born in Biran, Cuba.

Aug. 13, 1961
- Work began on Berlin Wall as East Germany sealed off the border between the city's eastern and western sectors in order to halt the flight of refugees.

Aug. 13, 2002
- In Nigeria the House of Representatives gave a two-week ultimatum to President Olusegun Obasanjo to resign of face Impeachment over alleged inadequacies.

Aug. 14, 1784
- The 1st Russian settlement in Alaska was established on Kodiak Island. Grigori Shelekhov, a Russian fur trader, founded Three Saints Bay.

Aug. 14, 1917
- The Chinese Parliament declared war on the Central Powers, Germany and Austria, during World War I.

Aug. 14, 1935
- U.S. President Franklin D. Roosevelt signed the Social Security Act into law. The act created unemployment insurance and pension Plans for the elderly.

DAYS OF HISTORY

Aug. 14, 1936
- The first basketball competition was held at the Olympic Games in Berlin, Germany. The U.S defeated Canada, 19-8.

Aug. 14, 1947
- Britain partitioned the subcontinent and Pakistan was founded as an independent country with Mohammed Ali Jinnah as president.

Aug. 14, 1989
- South African President P.W Botha announced his resignation after losing a bitter power struggle within his National Party.

Aug. 14, 2002
- Republic of Congo President Denis Sassou-Naguesso promised to fight corruption as he was sworn after winning this central African nation's first elections since back-to-back civil wars.

Aug. 15, 1057
- Macbeth, king of Scotland, was killed by Malcolm Canmore. He is best known as the subject of William Shakespeare' tragedy Macbeth and the many works it has inspired.

Aug. 15, 1824
- Freed American salves forms country of Liberia.

August 15, 1911
- Proctor & Gamble Company introduced Crisco vegetable Shortening.

August 15, 1947
- India declares independence from Uk, Islamic part becomes Pakistan

Aug. 15, 1948
- South Korea became the Republic of Korea.

Aug. 15, 2001
- Astronomers announced the discover of the first solar system outside our own.

Aug. 16, 1829
- The original Siamese twins, Eng and Chang, arrived in Boston to be exhibited to the western world.

Aug. 16, 1930
- The first British Empire Games were held at Hamilton, Ontario, Canada. The event is Now called the Commonwealth Games.

Aug. 16, 1960
- Cyprus, the third-largest island in the Mediterranean, became an independent republic.

Aug. 16, 1961
- Martin Luther King protested for black voting rights in Miami.

Aug. 16, 1979
- President Shehu Shagari was declared elected President of the Federal Republic of Nigeria.

Aug. 16, 2003
- Former Ugandan dictator Idi Amin died.

Aug. 17, 1863
- American Civil War: In Charleston, South Carolina, Union batteries and ships bombard Confederate-held Fort Sumter.

Aug. 17, 1950
Indonesia gains independence from Netherlands with Gabriel Leon M'Ba as president.

Aug. 17, 1994
- Riots break out in Lesotho as Motiotiehi (King) Letsie III dissolves the democratically elected Basotho Congress Party (BCP) government and Installs Hae Phoofolo as an interim prime minister.

DAYS OF HISTORY

Aug. 17, 1998
- President Bill Clinton admitted in taped grand jury Testimony (first president to do so). That he had had an "improper physical relationship" with Monica Lewinsky.

Aug. 18, 1968,
- Biafran separatists reject a Nigerian peace offer.

Aug. 1868
- French astronomer Pieme Jules Cesar Janssen discovers helium in the solar spectrum during an eclipse

Aug. 18, 1932
- The Scottish aviator Jim Mollison makes the first westbound transatlantic solo flight.

Aug. 18. 1977,
- The Federal Ministry of Internal Affairs announced that as at 1976. more than 74,000 foreign nationals were in the public and private establishment in Nigeria. A total of 113,827 foreigners visited the country while 528 persons were refused entry visas for various reasons, 137 repatriated for bad conduct and 19 others faced deportatiion order for various offences.

Aug. 19, 1692
- In Salem, Massachusetts, Province of Massachusetts bay five people, including a clergyman, are executed after being convicted of witchcraft.

Aug 19, 1888
- 1st beauty contest is held in Spa. Belgium. 18-years-old West Indian wins.

Aug 19, 1919
- Afghanistan gains full independence from the United Kingdom.

Aug. 19, 1946
- Bill Clinton, US President from 1992-2000, is born as William J. Blythe III in Hope, Arkansas. He was the son of Virginla Cassidy Blythe and William Jefferson Blythe II.

Aug. 19, 1969
- British army takes over policing of Northem Ireland.

Aug. 19, 1991
- Collapse of the Soviet Union, August Coup: Soviet President Mikhail Gorbachev is placed under house arrest while on holiday in the town
of Foros, Crimea.

Aug. 20, 1741
- Alaska was discovered by Danish navigator Vitus Jonas Bering. That's how the Bering Sea got its name.

Aug. 20, 1858
- Charles Darwin first publishes his theory of evolution in The Journal of the Proceedings of the Linnean Society of London, alongside Alfred Russel Wallace's same theory.

Aug. 20, 1866
- President Andrew Johnson formally declares of American Civil War over.

Aug. 20, 1920
- The first commercial radio station begins Operating in Detroit, Michigan with call sign 8MK (Now WWJ) (Newscadio 950). The radio station was started by The Detroit News newspaper and is now owned and run by CBS.

Aug. 20, 1960
- Senegal breaks from the Mali federation, declaring its independence.

DAYS OF HISTORY

Aug. 21, 1831
- Nat Turner led an insurrection of slaves in Virgina.

Aug. 21, 1841
- John Hampson of New Orleans patented the Venetian blind.

Aug. 21, 1878
- The American Bar Association was founded in Saratoga, N. Y.

Aug. 21, 1879
- The Virgin Mary, along with St. Joseph and St. John the Evangelist, reportedly appears to the people of knock, County Mayo, Ireland.

Aug. 21, 1888
- The first successful adding machine in the united States is patented by William Seward Burroughs.

Aug. 21, 1901
- The Cadillac Motor Company was formed in Detroit, Michigan, USA, named after the French explorer, Antoine Cadillac.

Aug. 21, 1985
- Tunisia expelled 253 Libyans in apparent retaliation for Libya's expulsion of over 20,000 Tunisian workers in recent weeks.

Aug. 21, 1991
- Latvia declared its independence from the Soviet Union.

Aug. 22, 1642
- The English Civil War began between supporters of King Charles I (Royalists or Cavaliers) and those of Oliver Cromwell (Roundheads)

Aug. 22, 1762
- Ann Franklin became the first woman to hold the title of newspaper editor. She assumed those duties at "The Newport Mercury" in Newport, RI.

Aug. 22, 1849
- The first air raid in history Austria launches pilotless balloons against the Italian city of Venice.

August 22, 1864
- Twelve nations sign the First Geneva Convention. The Red Cross is formed.

Aug. 22, 1901
- Cadillac Motor Company is founded.

August 22, 1902
- Theodore Roosevelt becomes the first President of the United States to ride in an automobile.

Aug. 22, 1911
- Mona Lisa stolen from Louvre (Recovered in 1913)

Aug. 24, 1858
- In Richmond, Virginia, 90 blacks are arrested for Learning.

Aug. 24, 1892
- Goodison Park in Liverpool, England, one of the world's first purpose-built football grounds. Opens.

Aug. 24, 1814
- The British set fire to the White House and the Capitol When they invaded Washington, DC during the War of 1812.

Aug. 24, 1934
- In Philadelphia, Pa., Philo T. Farnsworth (28) a
San Francisco scientist, produced use of television in astronomy.

Aug. 24, 1949
- The treaty creating North Atlantic Treaty Organization (NATO) goes into effect.

DAYS OF HISTORY

Aug. 24, 1954
- President Dwight D. Eisenhower signed the Act, virtually outlawing the communist Party in the United States.

Aug. 25, 1609
- Galileo demonstrates his first telescope to Venetian lawmakers.

Aug. 25, 1875
- Captain Matthew Webb became the first Person to swim across the English Channel. He made the swim from Dover to Cap Grisnez, France in 21 hours, 45minutes

Aug. 25, 1894
- Shibasaburo Kitasato discovers the infectious agent of the bubonic plague and publishes his findings in The Lancet.

Aug. 25, 1920
- Ethelda Bleibtrey became the first woman to win an event for the United States in Olympic competition. She won the 100-meter freestyle swimming competition at Antwerp, Belgium.

Aug. 25, 1964
- Kenneth David Kaunda wins Zambian elections and will become the first president of an independent republic on 24 October 1964.

Aug. 26, 1934
- Hitler's Nazi propaganda machine is now expelling foreign correspondents who place a slur or criticize Adolf Hitler and the latest is a US correspondent Dorothy Thompson.

Aug. 26, 1977
- The World conference for Action against Apartheid ended in Lagos after the delegates had signed a 32-point declaration condemning apartheid.

Aug. 26, 1977
- A high court in Ondo State ordered the Federal Electoral Commission to restore Mr. Afe Babalola as a candidate for the Ekiti Central Constituency in Ondo State.

Aug. 26, 1979
- Abel Tendekayi Muzorewa, who has been Prime Minister of the Republic of Rhodesia Since 1 June, announces that the country will be renames Zimbabwe.

Aug. 27, 1626
- The Danes were crushed by the Catholic League in Germany, marking the end of Danish intervention in European wars.

Aug. 27, 1789
- French National Assembly issued "Declaration of Rights of Man and Citizen."

Aug. 27, 1901
- In Havana, Cuba, U.S. Army Physician James Carroll allowed an infected mosquito to feed on him in an attempt to isolate the means of transmission of yellow fever.

Aug. 27, 1908
- Lyndon B. Johnson, the 36th president of the United States (1963-1969), was born near Stonewall, Texas.

Aug. 27, 1955
- The "Guinness Book of World Records" was 1st published. It posted sales of 80 million
in 1997.

Aug. 28, 1898
- Caleb Bradham renamed his carbonated soft drink 'Pepsi-Cola'.

Aug. 28, 1990
- Iraq declared Kuwait to be its newest province.

DAYS OF HISTORY

Aug. 28, 1991
- The Union of Socialist Soviet Republics collapsed and Mikhail Gorbachev resigned as Secretary of the Soviet Communist Party.

Aug. 28, 1963
- The March on Washington occurred as over 250,000 persons attended a Civil Rights rally in Washington, D.C., at which Rev. Dr. Martin Luther King, Jr. made his now-famous I Have a Dream speech.

Birthday German author-philosopher, Johann Wolfgang von Goethe (1749-1832), was born in Frankfurt am Main, Germany, He is best known for the dramatic poem Faust, completed in 1831.

Birthday The first American-born Roman Catholic saint, Elizabeth Ann Seton (1774-1821), was born (as Elizabeth Ann Bayley) in New York.
She founded the first American Catholic religious order, the Sisters of Charity of St. Joseph. In 1809, she opened an elementary school in Baltimore, marking the beginning of the parochial school system in the U.S.

Aug. 29, 1632
- English philosopher John Locke was born in Somerset.

Aug. 29, 1793
- Slaves in French colony of St. Domingue (Haiti) freed.

Aug. 29, 1831
- Micheal Faraday demonstrates first electric transformer.

Aug. 29, 1885
- Gottlieb Daimler patents the world's first motorcycle.

Aug. 29, 1885
- Boxing's first heavyweight title fight with 3-oz gloves and 3-minute rounds fought between John L Sullivan and Dominick McCaffrey

Aug. 29, 1898
- The Goodyear tire company is founded.

Aug. 29, 1966
- The Beatles played their last major live concert at Candlestick Park, California.

Aug. 29, 1998
- The G-34 transforms into a political party, Peoples' Democratic Party (PDP)

Aug. 30, 1918
- Lenin, new leader of Soviet Russia, shot and wounded after speech

Aug. 30, 1835
- Melbourne, Australia is founded.

Aug. 30, 1933
- Air France forms

Aug. 30, 1967
- Thurgood Marshall is confirmed as the first African American Justice of the United States Supreme Court.

Aug. 30, 1974
- A Belgrade-Dortmund express train derails at the main train station in Zagreb killing 153 passengers.

Aug. 30, 1983
- Guion S. Bluford Jr. became the first black American astronaut to travel in space, blasting off abroad the Challenger.

Aug. 30, 1999
- East Timor residents voted to secede from Indonesia.

DAYS OF HISTORY

Aug. 31, 1314
- King Hakon V Magnusson moves the capital of Norway from Bergen to Oslo.

Aug. 31, 1422
- Henry VI becomes King of England at the age of 9 months.

Aug. 31, 1897
- Thomas Edison patents the Kinetoscope, the first Movie projector.

Aug. 31, 1962
- The Caribbean nation of Trinidad and Tobago became Independent of British colonial rule.

Aug. 31, 1977
- Elections into Nigeria Constituent Assembly were held in 116 electoral colleges throughout the Federation, under peaceful atmosphere.

Aug. 31, 1997
- Diana, Britain's Princess of Wales, was killed in an early-morning car crash in Paris, France. Also killed was her millionaire companion, Harrods department store heir, Dodi Fayed.

Sept. 1, 1878
- Emma Nutt becomes the world's first female telephone operator when she was recruited by Alexander Graham Bell to the Boston Telephone Dispatch Company.

Sept. 1, 1906
- The International Federation of Intellectual Property Attorneys is established.

Sept. 1961
- The Eritrean War of Independence officially begins with the shooting of the Ethiopian police by Hamid Idris Awate.

Sept. 1, 1969
- A coup in Libya toppled the monarch of king Idris and borugh Muammar al Qaddafi to power

Sept. 1, 1977
- The Federal Government promulgated a new decree that any person who pays his income tax in one lump sum to cover tax liability of more than one year shall not be eligible to contest the election Into Constituent Assembly.

Sept. 2, 1666
- The Great Fire of London, having started at Pudding Lane, began to demolish about four-fifths of London Starting at the house of King Charles II's baker, Thomas Farrinor, after he forgot to extinguish his oven.

Sept. 2, 1930
- The first non-stop airplane flight from Europe to the US was completed as Captain Dieudonne Coste and Maurice Bellonte fo France arrived in Valley Stream, New York, aboard a Breguet Biplane.

Sept. 2, 1945
- The Japanese surrender delegation boarded the USS Missouri anchored in Tokyo Bay to formally sign documents of surrender, ending World War II

Sept. 2, 1989
- In Nicaragua, a 14-party opposition coalition chose Violeta Barrios de Chamorro as its presidential candidate. Chamorro went on to win the election the following February.

Sept. 3, 1590
- St. Gregory, he began his reign as Pope. Geogory the Great reigned until 604 and established the popes as the de facto rules of central Italy, and strengthened the papal primacy over the Churches of the West.

DAYS OF HISTORY

Sept. 3, 1777
- The American flag (stars & stripes), approved by Congress on June 14th, was carried into battle for the first time by a force under General William Maxwell.

Sept. 3, 1783
- The Treaty of Paris between the United States and Great Britain officially ended the Revolutionary War. The Treaty of 1783, which formally ended the American Revolution. Under the treaty, Great Britain recognized the independence of the United States.

Sept. 3, 1941
- Nazis made the 1st use of Zyclon-B gas in Auschwitz on Russian prisoners of war.

Sept. 4, 1781
- Los Angeles is founded by Spanish governor felipe De neve as Fl pueblo de Nuestra senora la Reina de los Angeles del Rio de Porciouncula (The Village of Our Lady, the Queen of Angels of the Porzioucola)

Sept. 4, 1802
- A French aeronaut dropped eight-thousand Feet Equipped with a Parachute.

Sept. 4, 1888
- George Eastman received patent # 388,850 for his roll-Film camera and registered his trademark: "Kodak." George Eastman introduced the box camera.

Sept. 4, 1904
- Dalai Lama signed a treaty allowing British commerce in Tibet.

Sept. 4, 1920
- Maggie Higgins, the first woman to win the Pulitzer Prize (1951) for international reporting, for her work in Korean War zones. Was born.

Sept. 4, 1957
- Ford Motor CO. introduced the 1958 Edsel. It was designed by Roy Brown and sold only 173,000 units through 1960.

Sept. 4 1977
- In Nigeria, The 19th bi-annual Convention of federation of Women Lawyer(FIDA) started at The National Theatre, Iganmu-Lagos.

Sept. 4, 1996
- In the Congo authorities found 200 slaughtered elephants in a marsh of the National Park of Odzalam.

Sept. 5, 1864
- Achille Francois Bazaine becomes Marshall of france.

Sept. 5, 1877
- Southern blacks led by Pap Singleton settle in Kansas.

Sept. 5, 1900
- France proclaims a protectorate over Chad.

Sept. 5, 1901
- Natioal Association of Professional Baseball Leagues forms.

Sept. 5, 1905
- The war in korea and Manchuria, between Japan and Russian ends.

Sept. 5, 1932
- The French Upper Volta is broken apart between Ivory Coast, Frence, sudan and Niger.

Sept. 6, 1899
- Carnation processes its first can of evaporated milk.

DAYS OF HISTORY

Sept. 6, 1901
- President William McKinley was shot by anarchist Leon Czolgosz at the Pan American Exposition in Buffalo, N.Y. McKinley died on September 14th

Sept. 6, 1949
- Allied military authorities relinquish control of former Nazi Germany assets back to German control.

Sept. 6, 1966
- In cape Town, South Africa, the architect of Apartheid, Prime Minister Hendrik Verwoerd, is stabbed to death during a parliamentary meeting.

Sept. 7, 1822
- Dom Pedro I declares Brazil independent from Portugal on the
shores of the Ipiranga creek in Sao Paulo.

Sept. 7, 1888
- Edith Eleanor McLean was the first baby to be placed in an Incubator. She weighed 2 pounds, 7 ounce. Originally, the incubator Hatching cradle.

Sept. 7, 1892
- The first world heavyweight title fight to use the Marquis of Queens berry Rules (including boxing gloves and three-minute Rounds) was held in New Orleans, LA. James Corbett knocked out
John L. Sullivan in round 21.

Sept. 7, 1893
_ The Genoa Cricket and Athletic Club, to become the first Italian
Football Club, is established by British expats.

Sept. 7, 1979
_ the Entertainment and Sports Programming Network(ESPN) made its debut on cable TV.

Sept. 8, 1914
-- World War 1: Private Thomas Highgate becomes the first British
soldier to be executed for desertion during the war.

Sept. 8, 1921
- 16-year-old Margaret Gorman wins the Atlantic City Pageant's Golden Mermaid trophy; pageant officials later dubbed her the first Miss America.

Sept. 8, 1924
- Alexandra Kollontal of Russia becomes first woman ambassador.

Sept. 8, 1926
- Germany is admitted to the League of Nations.

Sept. 8, 1951
- The San Francisco Peace Treat was signed, formally ending World War II hostilities with Japan.

Sept. 8, 1952
- East Hemmingway's "Old Man a,d Sea" published

Sept. 9, 1776
- The Second Continental Congress changed the name of the nation to the United State of America, from the United Colonies.

Sept. 9, 1948
- The People's Democratic Republicof Korea (North Korea)
Was created.

Sept. 9, 1967
- Uganda declares independence from Great British.

DAYS OF HISTORY

Sept. 9, 1976
- Chairman Mao Zedong, The Chinese revolutionary and statesman, has died in Beijing at the age of 82.

Sept. 9, 1990
- Liberia president Samuel K Deo is captured by Mr. Johnson's forces

Sept. 9, 1993
- The Palestine Liberation Organization officially recognizes Israel as a legitimate state.

Sept. 10, 1846
- Elias Howe of Massachusetts patents sewing machine.

Sept. 10, 1964
- Palestinian Liberation Arm(PLA) forms.

Sept. 10, 1967
- The people of Gibraltar vote to remain a British dependency rather than becoming part of Spain

Sept. 10, 1974
- Guinea Bissau, formally Guine Portuguesa, achieves Independence, the newly installed Chairman of the Council of State is Luis de Almeida Cabral.

Sept. 10, 1977
- Hamida Djandoubi, convicted of torture and murder, is the last person to be executed by guillotine in France.

Sept. 10, 2002
- Switzerland become the 190th member of the united Nations.

Sept. 12, 1910
- World's first female Cop, Alice Stebbins Well, appointed (Los Angeles Police Department).

Sept. 12, 1933
- Leo Szilard, waiting for a red light on Southampton Row in Bloodsbury, conceives the idea of nuclear chain reaction.

Sept. 12, 1943
- World War II: Benito Mussolini, dictator of Italy, is rescued From house arrest on the Gran Sasso in Abruzzi, by German Commando forces led by Otty Skorzeny.

Sept. 12, 1949
- Theodor House elected first President, Conrad Adenau first Prime Minister of West Germany.

Sept. 12, 1950
- Belgian government dismisses all communist civil servants.

Sept. 13, 1788
- The United State Philadelphia Convention sets the date for
The country's first presidential election, and New York City Becomes the temporary capital of the U.S.

Sept. 13 1881
- Lewis Latimer invented and patented an electric lamp with a carbon filament.

Sept. 13, 1899
- Henry Hale Bliss is the first United States to be killed in an auto Mobile accident, an electric taxi in Manhattan.

Sept. 13, 1914
- World War I: South African troops open hostilities is German South-West Africa(Namibia) with an assault on the Ramansdrift Police station.

Sept. 13, 1940
- Buckingham Palace was hit by German bombs causing superficial damage.

DAYS OF HISTORY

Sept. 14, 1901
- President of the United States William Mckinley dies after an assassination attempt on September 6, and is succeeded by Theodore Roosevelt.

Sept. 14, 1917
- Russia a officially proclaimed a republic.

Sept. 14, 1959
- The Soviet space probe Luna 2 become the first man-made object to reach the Moon when it crashed onto the lunar surface.

Sept. 14, 1960
- Coup under Col Joseph-Desire Mobutu in Congo, Army took control of the country just a few months after the country gains independence for Britain.

Sept. 14, 1960
- The Organization of the Petroleum Exporting Countries (OPEC) was founded by five core members:
Iraq, Iraq, Kuwait, Saudi Arabia, and Venezuela

Sept. 15, 1904
- Wilbur Wright makes his first airplane flight

Sept. 15, 1616
- The first non-airstocratic, free public school in Europe is opened in Frascati, Italy.

Sept. 15, 1857
- Timothy Alder patents typesetting machine

Sept. 15, 1928
- Alexander Fleming discovers penicillin

Sept. 15, 1952
- United Nations gives Eritrea to Ethiopia.

Sept. 15, 1981
- The Senate Judiciary Committee unanimously approves Sandra Day O'Connor to become the first female justice of the Supreme Court of the United States.

Sept. 16, 1795
- United Kingdom conquers Cape Town South Africa.

Sept. 16, 1941
- Concerned that Reza Pahlavi the Shan of Persia was about to align his petroleum-rich country with Germany during World War II, the United Kingdom
and the USSR occupy Iran and forced him to resign in favour of his son, Mohammad Reza Pahlavi.

Sept. 16, 1963
- Malaysia is formed from Malaya, Singapore, British North Borneo (Sabah) and Sarawak.

Sept. 16, 1975
- Papua New Guinea gains independence from Australia (National Day).

Sept. 16, 1975
- Cape Verda, Mozambique and Sao Tome and Principe
join the United Nations.

Sept. 17, 1787
- The Constitution of the United States of America was signed by delegates from twelve states at the Constitutions Convention in Philadelphia, PA.

Sept. 17, 1905
- Merrill W. Chase was born. Chase was an American immunologist who discovered cell mediated immunology. He discovered that white blood cells trigger the immune response in the body when an antigen appears.

DAYS OF HISTORY

Sept. 17, 1919
- German South West Africa is put under South African administration.

Sept. 17, 1985
- South African troops have invaded the neighbouring country of Angola to track down rebels fighting the Apartheid regime, they are also using rubber bullets, guns and tear gas on stone throwing student protesters increase across the country.

Sept. 18, 1759
- French Quebec surrendered to the British after the Sept. 13 battle on the Plains of Abraham, the last battle of the French and Indian Wars. French general
Montcalm and British general Wolfe died in the fray.

Sept. 18, 1850
Congress passed the Fugitive Slave Act, which required the return of escaped slaves to their owners.

Sept. 18, 1851
- First publication of The New-York Daily Times, which later becomes The New York Times.

Sept. 18, 1919
- The Netherlands gives women the right to vote.

Sept. 18, 1948
- Margaret Chase Smith of Maine becomes the first woman elected to the US Senate without completing another senator's term, when she defeats Democratic opponent Adrian Scolten.

Sept. 18, 1961
- U.N. Secretary-General Dag Hammarskjold dies in a plane crash while attempting to negotiate peace in the war-torn Katanga region of the Democratic Republic of the Congo.

Sept. 18, 1981
- Assemblee Nationale votes to abolish capital punishment in France.

Sept. 20, 1664
- Maryland passed the 1st anti-amalgamation law to stop intermarriage of English women and black men.

Sept. 20, 1842
- Lord James Dewar, physician who inverted the vacuum flask and cordite, the first smokeless powder, was born.

Sept. 20, 1850
- The slave trade in Washington, D.C., was abolished as a Provision of Henry Clay's Compromise of 1850. Because
each state had its own slavery code when the District of Columbia was founded in 1800, Washington had adopted Maryland's laws.

Sept. 20, 1859
- George Simpson patented the electric range.

Sept. 20, 1884
- If you thought equal rights for women is a modern Concept, think again. On this day, the Equal Rights Party was formed in San Francisco, California.

Sept. 21, 1677
- John and Nicolaas van der Heyden patents fire extinguisher

Sept. 21, 1784
- America's first daily paper, "The Pennsylvania Packet and Daily Advertiser". Was published in Philadelphia.

Sept. 21, 1792
- The National Convention declares France a Republic and abolishes the monarchy.

DAYS OF HISTORY

Sept. 21, 1949
- Federal Republic of (West) Germany created under 3-power occupation.

Sept. 21, 1949
- The Communist People's Republic of China is proclaimed under Mao Tse Tung.

Sept. 21, 1981
- Sandra Day O'Connor is unanimously approved by the U.S. Senate as the first female Supreme Court justice.

Sept. 22, 1692
- The last person was hanged for witchcraft in Salem, Massachusetts, United States.

Sept. 22, 1735
- Robert Walpole became the 1st British PM to live at 10 Downing Street.

Sept. 22, 1792
- The first French Republic was proclaimed.

Sept. 22, 1893
- The first American-made automobile, built by the Duryea Brothers, is displayed.

Sept. 22, 1908
- Bulgaria declared independence from Ottoman Empire (Turkey).

Sept. 22, 1960
- The Sudanese Republic is renamed Mali after the withdrawal of Senegal from the Mail Federation and became an independent republic.

Sept. 23, 1846
- Neptune is discovered by French astronomer Urbain Jean Joseph Le Verrier and British astronomer John Couch Adams; the discovery is verified by German Astronomer Johann Gottfried Galle.

Sept. 23, 1939
- Sigmund Freud, the founder of psychoanalysis, died in London.

Sept. 23, 1976
- South Africa decides to allow multi-racial teams to represent them.

Sept. 23, 1975
- In Nigeria, Mallam Adamu Ciroma was appointed the third Nigerian Governor of the Central Bank of Nigeria till June 27th, 1977. He later served as the Minister of Finance in the first term of President Olusegun Obasanjo democratic administration.

Sept. 23, 2002
- The first public version of the web browser Mozilla Firefox ("Phoenix 0.1") is released.

Sept. 24, 1657
- The first autopsy and coroner's jury verdict was Recorded in the state of Maryland.

Sept. 24, 1895
- First round-the world trip by a woman on a bicycle (took 15 months).

Sept. 24, 1903
- Alfred Deakin succeeds Edmund Baston as Australia Premier.

Sept. 24, 1956
- The first transatlantic telephone cable system from Newfoundland to Scotland began operation.

Sept. 24, 1973
- Guinea-Bissau declares its independence from Portugal.

Sept. 24, 1979
- CompuServe began operation as the first computer information service.

DAYS OF HISTORY

Sept. 24, 1990
- South African president F W de Klerk meets President Bush in Washington D.C.

Sept. 26, 1938
- Hitler issued his ultimatum to Czech government, demanding sudetenland

Sept. 26, 1941
- The U.S. Army established the Military Police Corps.

Sept. 26, 1950
- Indonesia was admitted to the UN.

Sept. 26, 1979
- Shagari declared president. In their one hour judgement read by Mr Justice Fatai Williams, the Supreme Court held that Alhaji Shehu Shagari was elected as the president of the Federation and returned by FEDECO in substantial compliance with the provision of section 34(1) (c)(11) of the
electoral decree.

Sept. 26, 1991
- AIDS patient Kimberly Bergalis pleaded with Congress to enact mandatory AIDS testing for health care workers.

Sept. 26, 1992
- A Nigerian military transport plane crashed Shortly after takeoff, killing all 163 people aboard.

Sept. 27, 1678
- "Pilgrim's Progress" by John Bunyan (b. 1628) is published.

Sept. 27, 1928
- Sir Alexander Fleming notices a bacteria-killing mould growing in his laboratory, discovering what later became
known as penicillin.

Sept. 27, 1981
- Joseph Paul Franklin, avowed racist, sentenced to life imprisonment for killing 2 black joggers in Salt Lake City.

Sept. 27, 1590
- Pope Urban VII dies 13 days after being chosen as the Pope, making his reign the shortest papacy in history.

Sept. 27, 1825
- The Stockton and Darlington Railway opens, and begins operation of the world's first service of Locomotive-hauled passenger trains.

Sept. 27, 1910
- First test flight of a twin-engined airplane (France)

Sept. 27, 1937
- Balinese Tiger declared extinct.

Sept. 27, 1992
- A Nigerian Air Force Hercules C-130 aircraft Crashes in Ejigbo outskirts of Lagos, Nigeria, killing 163 military personnel.

Sept. 27, 1967
- International Monetary Fund reforms world monetary system.

Sept. 27, 1998
- Google is established.

Sept. 28, 1785
- Napoleon Bonaparte (16) graduated from the military academy in Paris, He was 42nd in a class of 51.

Sept. 28, 1850
- Flogging was abolished as a form of punishment in the in the U.S. Navy.

Sept. 28, 1976
- Muhammad Ali kept his world heavyweight boxing Championship with a close 15-round decision over Ken Norton at New York's Yankee Stadium.

DAYS OF HISTORY

Sept. 28, 1976
- Muhammad Ali kept his world heavyweight boxing Championship with a close 15-round decision over Ken Norton at New York's Yankee Stadium.

Sept. 29, 1399
- King Richard II became the first English monarch to abdicate his throne.

Sept. 29, 1829
- The Metropolitan Police of London, later also known as the Met, is founded.

Sept. 29, 1895
- French chemist Louis Pasteur died.

Sept. 29, 1916
- John D. Rockefeller becomes the first billionaire.

Sept. 29, 1950
- Telephone Answering Machine created by Bell Laboratories.

Sept. 29, 1966
- Bechuanaland gains independence from England, becomes Botswana.

Sept. 30, 1912
- The Columbia School of Journalism opened in NYC, Joseph Pulitzer bequeathed $2 millionto start the school.

Sept. 30, 1960
- Fifteen African nations were admitted to the United Nations.

Sept. 30, 1962
- Black student James Meredith succeeded on his fourth try in registering for classes at the University of Mississippi. He became the first
black to enroll at Old Mississippi University and 13,500 Federal troops were required to back him up.

Sept. 30, 1999
- In Kenya Catholic bishops issued a pastoral letter that warned of civil arrest due to corruption, poverty and other problems. President Arap Moi was blamed for stalling constitutional reform.

Oct. 1, 1926
- An Oil field accident cost a famed American aviator, Wiley Post his left eye. But he used the settlement money to buy his first aircraft.

Oct. 1, 1949
- The People's Republic of China is declared by Mao Zedong.

Oct. 1, 1957
- The motto "In God We Trust" began appearing on US paper currency.

Oct. 1, 1960
- Nigeria gains independence from the United
Kingdom. (National Independence Day).

Oct 1, 1963
- In Nigeria Dr. Nnamdi Azikwe is sworn in as the Republic's first President by Sir Adetokunbo Ademola, the Chief Justice.

Oct. 1, 1971
- Walt Disney Productions opened its Magic Kingdom hin Orlando, Florida.

Oct. 3, 1922
- Rebecca L. Felton became the first woman U.S. Senator when she was appointed to serve out the term of Senator Thomas E. Watson.

Oct. 3, 1929
- The Kingdom of Serbs, Croats and Slovenes is renamed to Kingdom of Yugoslavia, "Land of the South Slaves"

DAYS OF HISTORY

Oct. 3, 1932
- Iraq gains Independence from the United Kingdom.

Oct. 3, 1977
- A 35-year-old legal practitioner, Mr. Godwin Agabi, was appointed the new chairman of the National Insurance Corporation of Nigeria. His appointment was for a period of three years.

Oct. 3, 1981
- The Hunger Strike by Provisional Irish Republican Army and Irish National Liberation Army prisoners at Maze prison in Northern Ireland ends after seven months and ten deaths.

Oct. 3, 1990
- East Germany and West Germany united to become Germany, 45 years after being split into two countries at the end of World War II.

Oct. 4, 1537
- The first complete English-language Bible (the Matthew Bible) is printed, with translations by William Tyndale and Miles Coverdale.

Oct. 4, 1830
- Provisional government declares secession of Belgium from Netherlands.

Oct. 4, 1957
- The first Earth satellite was launched into space this day by the Soviet Union. The craft circled the earth every 95 minutes at almost 2,000 miles per hour.
"Sputnik I" fell from the sky on January 4, 1958.

Oct. 4, 1966
- Basutoland becomes Independent from the United Kingdom and is renamed Lesotho.

Oct. 4. 1975
- A 50-man committee was set up to draft a new constitution for Nigeria in preparation for return to democracy in 1979.

Oct. 5, 1582
- Because of the implementation of the Gregorian calendar this day does not exist in this year in Italy, Poland, Portugal and Spain.

Oct. 5, 1880
- The first ball-point pen was patented on this day by Alonzo T. Cross.

Oct 5, 1916
- Adolf Hitler was wounded in WW I.

Oct. 5, 1944
- Suffrage is extended to women in France.

Oct. 5, 1958
- Racially desegregated Clinton High School in Clinton, Tenn., was mostly leveled by an early morning bombing.

Oct. 5, 1981
- President Ronald Reagan signed a resolution granting honorary American citizenship to Swedish diplomat Raoul Wallenberg, credited with saving about 100,000 Hungarians, most of them jews, from the Nazis during WW II.

Oct. 6, 1949
- The Soviet Union creates the Democratic Republic of Germany (East Germany) within the Soviet occupation zone.

Oct. 6, 1956
- Dr. Albert Sabin discovers oral Polio vaccine.

Oct. 6, 1977
- The Constituent Assembly began sitting in Lagos. The Membership totalled 230, some elected, others nominated.

DAYS OF HISTORY

Oct. 6, 1977
- Professor Sanya Onabamiro was appointed the chairman of the Implementation Committee for the National Policy on Education.

Oct 6, 1981
- Nobel Peace Prize-winner Anwar el-Sadat, the President of Egypt, was assassinated while reviewing a military parade. The attack was staged by Islamic Fundamentalists.

Oct 7, 1806
- Carbon paper patented in London by inventor Ralph Wedgewood.

Oct. 7, 1942
KLM, the flag carrier of the Netherlands, is founded. It is the oldest airline still operating under its original name.

Oct. 7, 1942
- U.S. and British government announce establishment of United Nations.

Oct. 7, 1949
- Wilhelm Pieck becomes First president of East Germany.

Oct. 7, 1960
- Nigeria joins the United Nations.

Oct 7, 1993
- Toni Morrison was awarded the Nobel Prize in literature. She was the first black woman to Receive the award and one of America's most significant novelists of the twentieth century.

Oct. 8, 1895
- Eulmi incident-Queen Min of Joseon, the last empress of Korea, is assassinated and her corpse burnt
by the Japanese in Gyeongbok Palace.

Oct. 8, 1945
- U. S. President Truman announced that only Britain and Canada would be given the secret to the atomic bomb.

Oct. 8, 1967
- Guerrilla leader Che Guevara and his men were captured in Bolivia.

Oct. 8, 1982
- In Poland, all labour organizations, including Solidarity, were banned.

Oct. 8, 1991
- A slave burial site was found by construction workers in lower Manhattan. The "Negro Burial Ground" had been closed in 1790. Over a dozen skeletons were found.

Oct. 8, 2003
- Arnold Schwarzenegger is elected the governor of California.

Oct. 9, 1701
- The Collegiate School of Connecticut (later renamed Yale University) is chartered in Old Saybrook, Connecticut

Oct. 9, 1875
- The sewing machine motor was patented by Isaac Singer (the Singer sewing maching guy) of New York.

Oct. 9, 1874
- World Postal Union forms in Bern, Switzerland

Oct. 9, 1930
- Aviator Laura Ingalls became the first Woman to make a solo transcontinental flight across the United States.

Oct. 9, 1963
- British premier Harold MacMillan, resigns

Oct. 9, 1967
- A day after being captured, Marxist revolutionary Ernesto "Che" Guevara is executed for attempting to incite a revolution in Bolivia

DAYS OF HISTORY

Oct. 9, 1970
- Khmer Republic (Cambodia) declares Independence

Oct. 9, 1981
- Abolition or capital punishment in France.

Oct. 9, 2004
- Afghanistan held its first democratic Election with an estimated 75 percent of the country's registered voter's casting votes

Oct. 10, 1846
- Neptune's moon Triton discovered by William Lasell

Oct. 10, 1865
- John Hyatts patents billard ball.

Oct. 10, 1868
- Carlos Cespedes issues the Grito de Yara from his plantation, La Demajagua, proclaiming Cuba's independence

Oct. 10, 1911
The Wuchang Uprising leads to the demise of Qing Dynasty, the last Imperial court in China, and the founding of the Republic of China.

Oct. 10, 1957
- US President Dwight D. Eisenhower apologizes to the finance minister of Ghana, Komla Agbeli Gbdemah, after he is refused service in a Dover, Delaware restaurant.

Oct. 10, 1964
- The United Progressive Grand Alliance (UPGA) published its manifesto for the 1964 Federal Election. With the publication, Nigeria's Federal election campaign had opened.

Oct. 10, 1978
- Daniel Arap Moi succeeds Kenyatta as president of Kenya.

Oct 11, 1795
- In gratitude for putting down a rebellion in the streets of Paris, France's National Convention appointed Napoleon Bonaparte second in command of the Army of the Army of the interior.

Oct. 11, 1811
- Inventor John Steven's first steam powered ferryboat, the Juliana, was put into operation between New York City and Hoboken, New Jersey.

Oct. 11, 1852
- The University of Sydney, Australia's oldest university is inaugurated in Sydney.

Oct. 11, 1868
- Thomas Edison patented his 1st invention, an electric voice machine.

Oct. 11, 1899
- South African Boars, settlers from the Netherlands, declared war on Great Britain.

Oct. 12, 1850
- First women's medical school (Women's Medical College of Pennsylvania, U.S.A),

Oct. 12, 1901
- President Theodore Roosevelt officially renames the "Executive Mansion" as the While House.

Oct. 12, 1928
- An iron lung respirator is used for the first time at children's Hospital, Boston

Oct. 12, 1968
- The games of the XIX Olympiad were opened in Mexico City by Mexican President Gustavo Diaz Ordaz. Norma Enriqueta Basilio de Sotelo became first woman to light the Olympic flame.

DAYS OF HISTORY

Oct. 12, 1984
- The Provisional Irish Republican Army bombs Hotels where Margaret Thatcher is staying, 5 die.

Oct. 13, 1892
- Edward Emerson Barnard discovers D/1892 T1, the first comet discovered by photographic means, on the night of October 13-14.

Oct. 13, 1914
- Garrett Morgan invents and patents gas mask

Oct. 13, 1923
- Ankara replaces Istanbul as the capital of Turkey.

Oct. 13, 1976
- The first electron micrograph of an Ebola viral Particle was obtained by Dr. F. A. Murphy, now at U. C. Davis, who was then working at the C. D. C.

Oct. 13, 1981
- Egypt's vice president Hosni Mubarak was elected president, one week after Anwar Sadat's assassination.

Oct. 13, 1983
- Ameritech Mobile Communications (now AT&T) launched the first US cellular network in Chicago, Ilinois.

Oct. 14, 1322
- Robert the Bruce of Scotland defeats King Edward II of England at Byland, forcing Edward to accept Scotland's independence.

Oct. 14, 1773
- The first recorded Ministry of Education, the Komisja Edukacji Narodewej (Polish for Commission of National Education), is formed in Poland.

Oct. 14, 1834
- First black to obtain a U. S. Patent, Henry Blair, for a corn planter.

Oct. 14, 1944
- German General Erwin Rommel or "the Desert Fox," is given the option of facing a public trial for treason, as a co conspirator in the plot to assassinate Adolf Hitler, or taking cyanide.

Oct. 14, 1964
- Martin Luther King, Jr., was awarded the Nobel Peace Prize for his work in civil rights.

Oct. 15, 1989
- South African ANC-founder/leader Walter Sisulu freed.

Oct. 15, 1987
- Coup in Burkina Faso, President Thomas Sankara dies.

Oct. 15, 1987
- Fiji becomes a republic, after belonging to Britain since 1874.

Oct. 15, 1992
- Charles Taylor launches an offensive against Monrovia Liberia.

Oct. 15, 1993
- Nelson Mandela and F. W. de Klerk were awarded the Nobel Peace Prize for their work to end apartheid in South Africa.

Oct. 15, 2003
- China became the third country to launch a staffed space mission.

Oct. 15, 2007
- The first Airbus Super jumbo, currently the largest passenger airliner in the world is delivered to Singapore Airlines.

DAYS OF HISTORY

Oct. 16, 1846
- The painkiller, ether, was demonstrated successfully for the first time in Boston's Massachusetts General Hospital. The drug was administered by William T.G. Morton, a 'dentist', of Charlestown. MA.

Oct. 16, 1847
- Charlotte Bronte's book "Jane Eyre" published

Oct. 16, 1934
- Chinese Communists begin the Long March; it ended a year and four days later, by which time Mao Zedong had regained his title as party chairman.

Oct. 16, 1940
- Benjamin O. Davis Sr. is named the first African American general in the United States Army.

Oct. 16, 1945
- The food and Agriculture Organization is founded in Quebec City, Canada.

Oct. 16, 1951
- The first Prime Minister of Pakistan, Liaquat Ali Khan, is assassinated in Rawalpindi.

Oct. 16, 1978
- Wanda Rutkiewicz is the first Pole and the first European woman to reach the summit of Mount Everest.

Oct. 16, 1991
- The National Republican Convention (NRC), and the Social Democratic Party (SDP), approved the list of candidates for the party primaries. A total of 414 aspirants would contest the election.

Oct. 17, 539 Bc
- King Cyrus The Great of Persia marches into the city of Babylon, releasing the Jews from almost 70 years of exile and making the first Human Rights Declaration.

Oct. 17, 1933
- Dr. Albert Einstein and is wife fleeing from Nazi Germany arrive in Princeton, New Jersey, where he will continue his scientific work at the Institute of Advanced Study.

Oct. 17, 1956
- The first commercial nuclear power Station is officially opened by Queen Elizabeth II in Sellafield, in Cumbria, England.

Oct. 17, 1977
- West German commandos storm hijacked Lufthansa in Mogadishu, Somalia Freeing all 86 hostages and killing 3 of 4 hijackers

Oct. 17, 1979
- Mother Teresa was awarded the Nobel Peace Prize for her work with the poor in Calcutta, India.

Oct. 18, 1867
- United States takes possession of Alaska after purchasing it form Russia for $7.2 million.

Oct. 18, 1922
- The British Broadcasting Company (later Corporation) is founded by a consortium, to establish a nationwide network of radio transmitters to provide a national broadcasting service.

Oct. 18, 1931
- Inventor Thomas Alva Edison died in West Orange, N.J., at age 84.

Oct. 18, 1968
- The U.S. Olympic Committee suspended two black athletes for giving a "black power" salute during a victory ceremony at the Mexico City games.

Oct. 18, 1977
- A Muslim leader in Nigeria, Alhaji Y. O. Shodeinde, Chief Imam of the Ahmadiyya Movement, supported the Government's decision to slash personal travelling allowance from N1000 to N500 for adults.

DAYS OF HISTORY

Oct. 19, 1722
- French C. Hopffer patents Fire extinguisher

Oct. 19, 1789
- Chief Justice John Jay is sworn in as the first Chief Justice of the United States.

Oct. 19, 1912
- Italy takes possession of Tripoli, Libya from the Ottoman Empire.

Oct. 19, 1933
- Basketball was introduced to the 1936 Olympic Games by the Berlin Organization Committee.

Oct. 19, 1943
- Streptomycin, the first antibiotic remedy for tuberculosis, is isolated by researchers at Rutgers University.

Oct. 19, 1986
- Samora Machel, President of Mozambique and a prominent leader of FRELIMO, and 33 others die when their Tupolev 134 plane crashes into the Lebombo Mountains

Oct. 20, 1820
- Spain sells part of Florida to U.S. for $5 million.

Oct 20, 1908
- King Leopold II sells Congo to Belgium

Oct. 20, 1935
- 400,000 demonstrated against fascism in Madrid.

Oct. 20, 1944
_ Liquid-gas tanks in Cleveland, Ohio, U. S. explodes, 135 die, 3,600 homeless.

Oct. 20, 1952
- Governor Evelyn Baring declares a state of emergency in Kenya and begins arresting hundreds of suspected leaders of the Mau Mau uprising, including Jomo Kenyatta, the future first President of Kenya.

Oct. 20, 1963
- South Africa begins trial of Nelson Mandela and 8 others on conspiracy

Oct. 20, 1970
- Siad Barre declares Somalia a socialist state.

Oct. 21, 1824
- Joseph Aspdin patents Portland cement (Yorkshire England)

Oct. 21, 1933
- Adolf Hitler withdraws Nazi Germany from the League of Nations

Oct. 21, 1949
- Harry S. Truman appoints the first female federal Judge in the nation. Burnita Shelton Matthews from Hazelhurst, MS

Oct. 21, 1950
- Death penalty abolished in Belgium

Oct. 21, 1959
- The Solomon R. Guggenheim Museum of modern and contemporary art, designed by architect Frank Lloysd Wright, opened to the public in New York City.

Oct. 21, 1997
- Elton John's tribute to Princess Diana, "Candle in the Wind 1997", was declared by "The Guinness Book of Records" to be the biggest-selling single record of all time. In 37 days, the single reached 31.8 million Copies sold.

DAYS OF HISTORY

Oct. 22, 1797
- One thousand meters (3,200 feet) above Paris, Andre-Jacques Garnerin makes the first recorded parachute jump.

Oct. 22, 1941
- World War II: French resistance member Guy Moquet and 29 other hostages are Executed by the Germans in retaliation for the death of a German officer.

Oct. 22, 1938
- Chester Carlson demonstrates first Xerox copying machine

Oct 22, 1954
West Germany joins North Atlantic Treaty Organization (NATO).

Oct. 22, 1964
- French philosopher/author Jean-Paul Sartre refuses Nobel Prize

Oct. 22, 1968
- Apollo program: Apollo 7 safely splashes down in the Atlantic Ocean after orbiting the Earth 163 times.

Oct. 23, 1707
- The first Parliament of Great Britain meets.

Oct. 23, 1775
- The Continental Congress approves a resolution barring free blacks from the army fighting for American independence from England.

Oct. 23, 1814
- British physician Joseph Constantine Carpue Perform the first major plastic surgery in the Western world (England)

Oct. 23, 1911
- First use of aircraft in war: An Italian pilot takes off from Libya to observe Turkish army lines during the TurcoItalian War.

Oct. 23, 1915
- Woman's suffrage: In New York City, 25,000-33,000 woman march on Fifth Avenue to advocate their right to vote.

Oct. 23, 1946
- The United Nations General Assembly convenes for the first time, at an auditorium in Flushing, Queens, New York City.

Oct. 23, 1947
- Husband and wife Dr. Carl Cori and Dr. Gerty Cori are first spouses to be awarded joint Nobel Prizes.

Oct. 23, 1973
- China and Japan formally ends four decades of dissension

Oct. 24, 1857
- Sheffield F.C., the world's first football club, is founded in Sheffield, England.

Oct. 24, 1901
- The first successful barrel ride over Niagara Falls occurred when Anna Edson Taylor, a school teacher, rode safely over the Falls today in a barrel. The ride through the rapids took is minutes

Oct. 24, 1964
- Northern Rhodesia gains independence from the United Kingdom and becomes the Republic of Zambia (Southern Rhodesia remained a colony)

Oct. 24, 2003
- Concorde makes its final commercial passenger flight, traveling at twice the speed of sound from New York City's John F. Kennedy International Airport to London's Heathrow Airport

Oct. 24, 2005
- Civil rights activist Rosa Parks died today of natural causes at the age of 92. Her refusal to give up her seat on a bus in Montgomery, Alabama, in 1955 triggered a bus boycott that Would mark the start of the modern civil rights Movement.

DAYS OF HISTORY

Oct. 25, 1400
- Geoffrey Chaucer, the author of the book Canterbury Tales, died in London.

Oct. 25, 1920
- After 74 days on Hunger Strike in Brixton Prison England, the Sinn Fein Lord Mayor of Cork, Terence MacSwiney died.

Oct 25, 1955
- The microwave oven was introduced in Mansfield, Ohio at the corporate headquarters of the Tappan Company.

Oct. 25, 1971
- The communist People's Republic of China is recognized by the United Nations and the Nationalist Chinese government of Taiwan is expelled.

Oct. 25, 1997
- After a brief civil war which has driven President Pascal Lissouba out of Brazzaville, Denis Sassou-Nguesso proclaims himself the President of the Republic of the Congo.

Oct. 26, 1863
- Worldwide Red Cross organized in Geneva

Oct. 26, 1950
- Mother Teresa founded her Mission of Charity in Calcutta, India.

Oct. 26, 1956
- UN's International Atomic Energy Agency statute approved.

Oct. 26. 1967
- John McCain a US Navy pilot in the Vietnam war, is shot down over North Vietnam and spends the next 5 1/2 years in prison, two of them in solitary confinement.

Oct. 26, 1974
- Mathieu Kerekou (b. 1933) seized power in Dahomey (later Benin) and ruled until 1991. He was elected president in 1996 and served until 2006.

Oct. 26, 1979
- South Korean president Park Chung He was killed by the head of the Korean Central Intelligence Agency.

Oct. 27, 1492
- Christopher Columbus discovers Cuba and claims it for Spain.

Oct. 27, 1811
- Isaac Merrit Singer, born in Pittstown, New York, was the English inventor of the continuous-stitch sewing machine in 1851.

Oct. 27, 1922
- A referendum in Rhodesia rejects the country's annexation to the South African Union.

Oct. 27, 1938
- Dupont announces its new synthetic fiber will be called 'nylon.'

Oct. 27, 1958
- Iskander Mirza, the first President of Pakistan, is deposed in a bloodless coup d'etat by Gen. Ayub Khan, who had been appointed the enforcer of martial law by Mirza 20 days earlier.

Oct. 28, 1914
- George Eastman of the 'Kodak' company, Announces the invention of colour photographs

Oct. 28, 1922
- Italian fascists led by Benito Mussolini march on Rome and take over the Italian government.

DAYS OF HISTORY

Oct. 28, 1948
- Swiss chemist Paul Muller is awarded the Nobel Prize in Physiology or Medicine for his discovery of the insecticidal properties of DDT.

Oct. 28, 1949
- Eugenie Anderson is first woman U.S. ambassador

Oct. 28, 1954
- Ernest Hemingway wins Nobel Prize for literature

Oct. 28, 2007
- Cristina Fernandez de Kirchner becomes the first Woman elected President of Argentina.

Oct. 29, 1923
- Turkey becomes a republic following the dissolution of the Ottoman Empire.

Oct. 29, 1957
- Israel's Prime Minister David Ben Gurion and five of his ministers are injured when a hand grenade is tossed into Israel's parliament, the Knesset.

Oct. 29, 1958
- The first Implantable heart pacemaker was inserted into the chest of Swedish cardiac patient Arne Larson in Stockholm.

Oct. 29, 1960
- In Louisville, Kentucky, Cassius Clay (who later takes the name Muhammad Ali) Wins his first professional fight, beats Tunney Hunsaker.

Oct. 29, 1961
- Syria seceded from the United Arab Republic to form the Syrian Arab Republic.

Oct. 30, 1888
- John J Loud patents ballpoint pen

Oct. 30, 1894
- The time clock was patented by Daniel M. Cooper of Rochester, NY.

Oct. 30, 1905
- Aspirin developed by the German Company Bayer

Oct. 30, 1953
Gen. George C. Marshall won the Nobel Peace Prize for originating the Marshall Plan.

Oct. 30, 1960
Michael Woodruff performs the first successful Kidney transplant in the United Kingdom at the Edinburgh Royal Infirmary.

Oct. 30, 1974
- Muhammad Ali knocked out George Foreman in the eighth round of a 15-round bout in Kinshassa, Zaire ("rumble in the jungle") to regain his world heavyweight title.

Oct. 30, 1947
- The General Agreement on Tariffs and Trade Organisation (WTO), is founded.

Oct. 30, 1991
- A US Federal Judge in Boston ordered the American Customs Service to pay a Nigerian woman, Mrs. A. Adedeji 215,000 dollars for a humiliating strip and body cavity search without warrant or reasonable belief of illegal acts.

Oct. 30, 1995
- Quebec votes against separation from Canada by 50.6 per cent to 49.4 per cent.

Oct. 31, 1795
- John Keats, British poet, born on this day ("On a Grecian Urn, Ode to a Nightingale, Ode to Autumn; died Feb. 23, 1821)

DAYS OF HISTORY

Oct. 31, 1815
- Sir Humphrey Davy of London patents miner's safety lamp

Oct. 31, 1888
- John Boyd Dunlop patents pneumatic bicycle tyre

Oct. 31, 1892
- Arthur Conan Doyle publishes The Adventures of Sherlock Holmes.

Oct. 31, 1908
- 4th Olympic Games ends in London

Oct. 31, 1937
- Spanish government moves from Valencia to Barcelona.

Oct. 31, 1956
Rear Admiral G. J. Dufek became the first person to land and airplane at the South Pole.

Oct. 31, 1992
- Roman Catholic Church, reinstates Galileo Galilei after 359 years

Nov. 1, 1800
- US President John Adams becomes the first President of the United States to live in the Executive Mansion (later renamed the White House).

Nov. 1, 1894
- Vaccine for diphtheria announced by Dr. Roux of Paris.

Nov. 1, 1945
- First issue of Ebony magazine published by John H. Johnson.

Nov. 1, 1957
- World longest suspension bridge opens in Mackinac Straits, Michigan.

Nov. 1, 1977
- Nigeria's N28 million giant oil tanker, MV Oloibiri, sailed into her territorial waters for the first time and was welcomed by a government delegation led by the Chief of Staff Supreme Headquarters Brigadier Musa Yar'Adua.

Nov. 1, 1993
- The Maastricht Treaty takes effect, formally establishing the European Union.

Nov. 2, 1930
- Haile Selassie is crowned Emperor of Ethiopia at Addis Ababa's Cathedral of St. George in a lavish ceremony attended by royals and dignitaries from all over the world.

Nov. 2, 1936
- First high-definition TV broadcast service,
by BBC in London.

Nov. 2, 1976
- Jimmy Carter defeated Gerald Ford, becoming the first U.S. president from the deep South since the Civil War.

Nov. 2, 1983
- President Ronald Reagan signs a bill in the White House Rose Garden designating a federal holiday honouring the civil rights leader Martin Luther King, Jr., to be observed on the third Monday of January.

Nov. 3, 1838
- The Times of India, the world's largest circulated English language daily Broadsheet newspaper is founded as The Bombay Times and Journal of Commerce.

Nov. 3, 1911
- Chevrolet officially enters the automobile market in competition with the Ford Model T.

DAYS OF HISTORY

Nov. 3, 1952
- Egypt protests German retribution payments to Israel.

Nov. 3, 1955
- The first crystallised virus is announced.

Nov. 3, 1961
- President John F. Kennedy establishes the US Agency for International Development.

Nov. 3, 1978
- Dominica gains independence from Britain.

Nov. 4, 1846
- Benjamin F. Palmer of Meredith N. H. received a patent on an artificial human leg.

Nov. 4, 1904
- Harvard Stadium became the first stadium built specifically for football.

Nov. 4, 1975
- Fidel Castro orders the deployment of Cuban troops in Angola in order to aid the Marxist MPLA-ruled government against the South African-backed UNITA opposition forces.

Nov. 4, 1995
- Israeli Prime Minister Yitzhak Rabin, 73-years-old, was killed by a right-wing 27-years-old Israeli law Yigal Amir, at a Tel Aviv peace rally. Shimon Peres assumed the post of acting Prime Minister.

Nov. 4, 1998
- Brazil set a minimum retirement age of 53 for men and 48 for women.

Nov. 5, 1492
- Christopher Columbus learned of maize (corn) from the Indians of Cuba.

Nov. 5, 1789
- French National Assembly declared all citizens equal under law.

Nov. 5, 1800
- Napoleon surrenders Malta to Great Britain.

Nov. 5, 1895
- George Selden patents first Gasoline-driven car.

Nov. 5, 1925
- Mussolini disbands Italian socialist parties.

Nov. 5, 1932
- The French Upper Volta is broken apart between Ivory Coast, French Sudan, and Niger.

Nov. 5 1840
- Afghanistan surrendered to the British.

Nov. 5, 1946
- U. S. Republicans took control of the Senate and the House in midterm elections.

Nov. 6, 1856
Scenes of Clerical Life, the first work of fiction by the author later known as George Eliot, is submitted for publication.

Nov. 6, 1913
Life, the first work of fiction by the author later known as Geoge Eliot, is submitted for publication.

Nov. 6, 1928
- Jacob Schick patents first electric razor

Nov. 6, 1935
- Parker Brothers acquires the forerunner patents for MONOPOLY from Elizabeth Magie.

DAYS OF HISTORY

Nov. 6, 1944
- Plutonium is first produced at the Hanford Atomic Facility and subsequently used in the Fat Man atomic bomb dropped on Nagasaki, Japan.

Nov. 1985
- In Colombia, leftist guerrillas of the April 19 Movement seize control of the Palace of Justice in Bogota, eventually killing 115 People, 11 of them Supreme Court justices.

Nov. 6, 1979
- Ayatolla Khomeini takes over in Iran

Nov. 6, 1999
- Australians vote to keep the Head of the Commonwealth as their head of state in the Australian republic referendum.

Nov. 7, 1665
- The London Gazette, the oldest surviving journal, is first published.

Nov. 7, 1775
- John Murray, the Royal Governor of the Colony of Virginia, starts the first mass emancipation of salves in North America by issuing Lord Dunmore's Offer of Emancipation, which offers freedom to slaves who abandoned their colonial masters in order to fight with Murray and the British.

Nov. 7, 1876
The cigarette manufacturing machine was patented by Albert H. Hook of New York City.

Nov. 7, 1916
- Jeannette Rankin is the first woman to elected to the United States Congress.

Nov. 7, 1990
- Mary Robinson becomes the first woman to be elected President of the United States Congress.

Nov. 7, 2000
- Hillary Rodham Clinton is elected to the United States Senete, becoming the first former First Lady to win public office in the United States, although actually she still was the First Lady.

Nov. 8, 1520
- Stockholm Bloodbath begins: A successful invasion of Sweden by Danish forces results in the execution of around 100 people.

Nov. 8, 1793
- In Paris, the French revolutionary government opens the Louvre to the public as a museum.

Nov. 8, 1829
- Lord William Bentinck, Governor-General of the East India Company, called for the abolition of sati (suttee), the practice of a widow burning herself to death on her husband's funeral pyre.

Nov. 8, 1895
- William Rontgen discovered electromagnetic Radiation in a wavelength range known as X-rays during an experiment at the University of Wurzburg.

Nov. 9, 1848
- Robert Blum, a German revolutionary, is executed in Vienna.

Nov. 9, 1921
- Albert Einstein receives the Nobel Prize in Physics "for his services to Theoretical Physics, and especially for his discovery of the law of the photoelectric effect."

Nov. 9, 1970
- Former French president Charles De Gaulle died at age 79.

DAYS OF HISTORY

Nov. 9, 1989
- The 27.9-mile-long Berlin Wall, the symbol of the Cold War that separated East and West Germany for 28years, was opened. Both East and West German citizens celebrated their freedom as they once again were able to walk freely.

Nov. 10, 1885
- Gottlieb Daimler's motorcycle, world's first, unveiled

Nov. 10, 1891
- Granville T. Woods patents Electric railway

Nov. 10, 1952
- Trygve Halvdan Lie resigns as first secretary-general of UN.

Nov. 10, 1969
- Sesame Street known for its Muppet Characters, created by the late Jim Henson makes its debut on PBS.

Nov. 10, 1989
- Germans begins demolishing Berlin Wall.

Nov. 10, 1995
- In Nigeria, playwright and environmental activist Ken Saro-Wiwa, along with eight others from the Movement for the Survival of the Ogoni People (Mosop), are hanged by government forces, despite worldwide pleas for clemency.

Nov. 11, 1918
- Independence Day is celebrated in Poland to commemorate the restoration of Poland as a sovereign democratic state after 123 years of partitions.

Nov. 11, 1965
- Rhodesia proclaimed independence from Britain by PM Ian D Smith.

Nov. 11, 1969
- George R. carruthers patented an image Converter for detecting electromagnetic radiation.

Nov. 11, 1975
- The African nation of Angola was proclaimed independent.

Nov. 11, 1994
- Bill Gates buys Leonardo da Vinci's "Codex" for $30,800,000.

Nov. 11, 2004
- Yasser Arafat is confirmed dead by the Palestine Liberation Organization, of unidentified causes. Mahmoud Abbas is elected chairman of the PLO minutes later.

Nov. 12, 1793
- Jean Sylvain Bailly, the first Mayor of Paris, is guillotined.

Nov. 12, 1847
- Sir James Young Simpson, a British physician, is the first to use chloroform as an anaesthetic.

Nov. 12, 1927
- Leon Trotsky was expelled from the Communist Party and Joseph Stalin became the ruler of the Soviet Union.

Nov. 12, 1945
- Nobel Peace Prize awarded to Cordell Hull for his role in establishing the United Nations.

Nov. 12, 1997
- Ramzi Yousef is found Guilty of masterminding the 1993 World Trade Center bombing.

Nov. 12, 1990
- Sir Tim Berners-Lee with Help from Robert Cailliau Publish a formal proposal for the World Wide Web on this day in History.

DAYS OF HISTORY

Nov. 13, 1841
- James Braid first sees a demonstration of animal magnetism, which leads to his study of the subject he eventually calls hypnotism.

Nov. 13, 1839
- First U. S. anti-slavery party, Liberty Party, convenes in NY

Nov. 13, 1940
- The prototype for the Jeep featuring four-wheel drive, an open-air cab, and a rifle rack mounted under the windshield was submitted to the U. S. Army for approval by the car maker Willys-Overland. One year later, with the U. S. declaration of war, mass production of the Jeep began. By the war's end in 1945, some 600,000 Jeeps had rolled off the assembly lines.

Nov. 13, 1947
- Russia completes development of the AK-47, one of the first proper assault rifles.

Nov. 13, 1971
- The American space probe. Mariner 9, Becomes the first spacecraft to orbit another planet successfully, swinging into its planned trajectory around Mars.

Nov. 13, 1994
- In a referendum votes in Sweden decide to join the European Union.

Nov. 13, 1997
- U. N. pulls out arms inspection teams from Iraq

Nov. 14, 1889
Pioneering female journalist Nellie Bly (aka Elizabeth Cochrane) begins a successful attempt to travel around the attempt to travel around the world in lessthan 80 days. She completes the trip in seventy-two days.

Nov. 14, 1922
- The British Broadcasting Company begin broadcasting on medium wave, from Marconi House in London with the first newscast.

Nov. 14, 1969
- Apollo program: NASA launches Apollo 12, the second manned mission to the surface of the Moon.

Nov. 14, 1985
- A volcano erupted in Colombia, sending floods of mud and water into the nearby river. The lava from this volcanic eruption buried an entire town of people along with three villages.

Nov. 14, 2002
Nancy Pelosi of California became the first Woman to lead a party in Congress.

Nov. 14, 2003
The most distant object ever found in our solar System, named Sedna, was discovered by astronomers at the Mount Palomar Observatory.

Nov. 15, 1904
- King C Gillette patents Gillette razor blade.

Nov. 15, 1920
- First assembly of the League of Nations is held in Geneva.

Nov. 15, 1945
- Nathuram Godse and Narayan Apte are executed for assassinating Mahatma Gandhi.

Nov. 15, 1977
- The Head of State, Lt. General Olusegun Obasanjo, Inaugurated a new Federal Electoral Commission at the Nigerian Institute of International Affairs in Lagos. The 24-man Commission, including four women federal representatives, was appointed on October 22 with a retired civil servant, Mr. Richard Ani, as chairman.

DAYS OF HISTORY

Nov. 15, 1991
- Twenty-five years after the position of Sarduana of Sokoto became vacant. Finance and Economic Development Minister, Alhaji Abubakar Alhaji was turbaned the new Sardauna.

Nov. 16, 1945
- United Nations Educational, Scientific and Cultural Organization (UNESCO) is founded.

Nov. 16, 1977
- President Julius Nyerere of Tanzania arrived in Lagos to begin a five-day State visit to Nigeria during which he talks with Lt. General Olusegun Obasanjo, particularly on the liberation Struggles in Southern Africa.

Nov. 16, 1997
- After nearly 18 years of incarceration, the People's Republic of China releases Wei Jingsheng, a pro-democracy dissident, From jail for medical reasons.

Nov. 16, 1998
- The Federal High Court, Lagos, awards N2.5m as damages to Obose Igiebor, daughter of TELL magazine's editor-in-chief, Mr. Nosa Igiebor and her mother, for the unlawful and her unconstitutional invasion of their residence by the Federal Government security agents in 1997.

Nov. 17, 1800
- John Adams is the first President to move into the White House.

Nov. 17, 1855
- David Livingstone becomes the first European to see the Victoria Falls in what is now present-day Zambia-Zimbabwe.

Nov. 17, 1947
- American scientists John Bardeen and Walter Brattain observe the basic principles of the transistor, a key element for the electronics revolution of the 20th Century.

Nov. 17, 1970
- The soviet Union's moon over rolled over the moon's surface today, becoming the first roving remote-controlled robot to land on the moon.

Nov. 17, 1970
- Douglas Engelbart receives the patent for The first computer mouse.

Nov. 18, 1493
- Christopher Columbus first sighted the Island Now known as Puerto Rico.

Nov. 18, 1626
- Pope Urban VIII consecrated adopted a system of Standard Time zones. The railroad companies got together and established standard railroad time to increase safety and surmount complex scheduling on local times to increase safety and surmount complex scheduling on local times. This put an end to "God's time."

Nov. 18, 1918
- Latvia declared its independence from Russia.

Nov. 18, 1958
- The first true reservoir in Jerusalem opened.

Nov. 18, 1963
- The first push-button telephone went into service.

Nov. 19, 1493
- Christopher Columbus goes ashore on an Island he first saw the day before. He names it San Juan Bautista (later renamed Puerto Rico).

Nov. 19, 1703
- the "Man in the Iron Mask," a prisoner in Bastille prison in Paris, died.

DAYS OF HISTORY

Nov. 19, 1794
- The United States and Britain signed the Jay Treaty, which resolved some issues left over from the Revolutionary War. This was the 1st US extradition treaty.

Nov 19, 1816
- Warsaw University was established.

Nov. 19, 1928
- The 1st issue of Time Magazine featured Japanese Emperor Hirohito on cover.

Nov. 19, 1946
- Afghanistan, Iceland and Sweden Joined the United Nations.

Nov. 20, 1920
- Nobel Peace Prize awarded to U.S. president Woodrow Wilson.

Nov. 20, 1923
Garrett Morgan invents and patents traffic signal.

Nov. 20, 1945
- The war crimes trials of 24 German World War II leaders began in Nuremberg, Germany.

Nov. 20, 1959
U. N. adopts Universal Declaration of Children's Rights.

Nov. 20, 1968
Methane gas explosions in a West Virginia Coal mine kills 78 men.

Nov. 20, 1969
- Soccer star Pele collected his 1,000th Career goal in Rio de Janeiro.

Nov. 20, 1970
- U. N. General Assembly accepts membership of China PR

Nov. 20, 1977
- Egyptian President Sadat became 1st Arab leader to address Israeli Knesset.

Nov. 20, 1992
- Fire damages a major part of Windsor Castle and a number of important works of art, books and furniture are lost some through fire damage but also many through water damage caused by the 35 fire engines that fought the fire.

Nov. 20, 1994
- The Angolan government and UNITA rebels sign the Lusaka Protocol in Zambia, ending 19 years of civil war (localized fighting resumes the next year).

Nov. 21, 1791
- Colonel Napoleon Bonaparte is promoted to full general and appointed Commander-in-Chief of the Armies of the French Republic.

Nov. 21, 1877
- Thomas Edison announces his invention of the phonograph, a machine that can record and play sound.

Nov. 21, 1918
- Flag of Estonia, previously used by pro-independence activists, is formally adopted as national flag of the Republic of Estonia.

Nov. 21, 1962
- China agreed to a cease-fire on India-China border.

Nov. 21, 1974
- The Freedom of Information Act was passed by US Congress over President Ford's veto.

Nov. 21, 1977
- The 1st commercial flight of the Anglo-French Concorde jet was from London to Bahrain.

DAYS OF HISTORY

Nov. 22, 1497
- Portuguese explorer Vasco de Gama became the first navigator Sail around the Cape of Good Hope in his search for a sea route to India.

Nov. 22, 1963
- President John F. Kennedy was assassinated when he was shot by a sniper while riding in a motorcade through downtown Dallas.

Nov. 22, 1967
- UN Security Council Resolution 242 is adopted by the UN Security Council, establishing a set of the principles aimed at guiding negotiations for an Arab-Israeli peace settlement.

Nov 23, 1868
- Louis Ducos du Hauron Patents trichrome colour Photo process

Nov. 23, 1897
- pencil sharpener patented by J L Love

Nov. 23, 2001
- Convention on Cybercrime is elected president of Liberia and becomes the first woman to lead and African country.

Nov. 24, 1914
- Benito Mussolini left Italy's Socialist party.

Nov. 24, 1965
- Joseph Desire Mobutu Seizes power in the Congo and becomes President; he rules the country (which he renames Zaire in 1971) for over 30 years, until being overthrown by rebels in 1997

Nov. 24, 1989
- Romanian leader Nicolae Ceausescu was unanimously re-elected Communist Party chief Within a month, he was overthrown in a popular uprising and executed along with his wife, Elena, on Christmas Day.

Nov. 26, 1865
- "Alice in Wonderland" by Lewis Carroll published in US.

Nov. 26, 1949
- The Indian Constituent Assembly adopts india's Constitution presented by Dr. B. R. Ambedkar.

Nov. 26, 1977
- The Supreme Military Council announced the Appointment of Mr. Justice Dan Ibekwe, hitherto the Attorney-General and Federal Commissioner for Justice as President of the newly-created Federal Court of Appeal.

Nov. 27, 1895
- Alfred Nobel signs his last will and testament, setting aside his estate to establish the Nobel Prize after he dies.

Nov. 27, 1912
- Spain declares a protectorate over the north shore of Morocco.

Nov. 27, 1963
- The Convention on the unification of Certain Points of Substantive Law on Patents for Invention is signed at Strasbourg.

Nov. 27, 1971
- The Soviet space program's Mars 2 Orbiter releases a descent module. It Malfunctions and crashes, but it is the first man-made object to reach the surface of Mars.

Nov. 27, 1991
- The United Nations Security Council Resolution 721, leading the way to the establishment of peacekeeping operations in Yugoslavia.

DAYS OF HISTORY

Nov. 27, 2001
- A hydrogen atmosphere is discovered on the extrasolar planet Osiris by the Hubble Space Telescope, the first atmosphere detected on an extrasolar detected on an extrasolar planet.

Nov. 27, 2005
- The first partial human face transplant is Completed in Amiens, France.

Nov. 28, 1814
- The Times in London is for the first time printed by automatic, steam powered presses built by the German inventors Friedrich Koenig and Andreas Friedrich Bauer, signaling the beginning of the availability of newspapers to mass audience.

Nov. 28, 1628
- John Bunyan, born on this day (author: A Pilgrim's Progress, Grace Abounding, The Life and Death of Mr. Badman, The Holy War; died in 1688)

Nov. 29, 1890
- The Meiji Constitution goes into effect in Japan and the first Diet convenes.

Nov. 29, 1899
- Spanish football club FC Barcelona is founded by Joan Gamper.

Nov. 29, 1910
- The first US patent for inventing the traffic lights System is issued to Emest E. Sirrine.

Nov. 29, 1944
- In Johns Hopkins hospital, Alfred Blalock and Vivien Thomas, a black assistant performed the 1st open heart surgery.

Nov. 29, 1962
- Algeria banned the Communist party.

Nov. 30, 1782
- Provisional articles of peace are signed in Paris between Britain and the United States, under which Britain recognizes U. S. Independence.

Nov. 30, 1872
- The first-ever international Football match took place at Hamilton Crescent, Glasgow, Between Scotland and England.

Nov. 30, 1954
- Johannes Gerhardus Strijdom is elected premier of South Africa. Strijdom's Extreme policies resulted in the removal of Coloureds from the common voters roll and the extended 'treason trial' of 156 activists (including Nelson Mandela) involved in the Freedom Charter.

Dec. 1, 1918
- The kingdom of Serbs, Croats and Slovenes (later known as the Kingdom of Yugoslavia) is proclaimed.

Dec. 1, 1959
- Twelve nations, including the United States, sign a treaty setting aside Antarctica as a scientific preserve free from military activity.

Dec. 1, 1982
- At the University of Utah, Barney Clark becomes the First person to receive a permanent artificial heart.

Dec. 1, 1997
- Representatives from more than 150 countries gathered at a global warming summit in Kyoto, Japan, and over the Course of 10 days forged an agreement to control the emission of greenhouse gases.

Dec. 2, 1804
- Napoleon Bonaparte was Crowned emperor of France in Paris by Pope Pius VII

DAYS OF HISTORY

Dec. 2, 1942
- An artificially created, self-sustaining nuclear chain reaction was demonstrated For the first time, at the University of Chicago.

Dec. 2, 1971
- The United Arab Emirates (UAE) is formed as a federation from the seven emirates of Abu Dhabi, Ajman, Dubai, Fujairah, Ras al-Khaimah, Sharjah, and Umm al-Quwain becoming one United country, which has evolved into a modern, high-income nation.

Dec. 3, 1910
- The neon lamp was displayed for the first time at the Paris Motor Show. The lamp was developed by French physicist Georges Claude.

Dec. 3, 1922
- The first successful Technicolor motion picture, "The Toll of the Sea", was shown at the Rialto Theatre in New York City.

Dec. 3, 1963
- Nelson Mandela's treason trial begins in South Africa.

Dec. 3, 1976
- An assassination attempt is made on Bob Marley. He is Shot twice, but plays a concert Two days later.

Dec. 4, 1812
- Peter Gaillard of Lancaster, Pennsylvania patents a horse-drawn mower

Dec. 4, 1833
- American Anti-Slavery Society formed by Arthur Tappan in Philadelphia.

Dec. 4, 1843
- Manila paper (made from sails, canvas and rope) patented, mass

Dec. 4, 1864
- Romanian Jews are forbidden to practice law

Dec. 4, 1958
- Dahomey (present-day Benin) Becomes a self-governing country within the French Community.

Dec. 4, 1977
- Malaysia Airlines flight 653 is hijacked and crashes in Tanjong Kupang, Johor, killing 100.

Dec. 4, 1991
- Journalist Teny A. Anderson is released after 7 Years in captivity as a hostage in Beirut. He was the last and Longest-held American hostage in Lebanon.

Dec. 4, 1991
- Pan American World Airways (Pan AM) takes it's last commercial Pan Am Flight 436 from Bridgetown. Barbados, to Miami. Pan Am is remembered for being the first worldwide mail delivery service on Aircraft called Clipper flying boats, and created many firsts including the first commercial service across the North Atlantic.

Dec. 4, 1993
- A truce is concluded between the government of Angola and UNITA rebels.

Dec. 5, 1868
- The first American bicycle School opened in New York City. It announced courses for Velocipede riding.

Dec. 5, 1909
- George Taylor makes the first manned glider flight in Australia in a glider that he designed himself.

Dec. 5, 1924
- Robert Mangaliso Sobukwe, leader of South Africa's Pan Africanist Congress, PAC was born.

DAYS OF HISTORY

Dec. 5, 1951
- The first push button-controlled garage opened in Washington, DC. A single attendant without entering a car, could automatically park or return an auto to or from the 'Park-O-Mat' in less than a minute.

Dec. 6, 1768
- First edition of "Encyclopedia Brittanica" published (Scotland).

Dec. 6, 1790
- The U.S. Congress moves from New York City to Philadelphia, Pennsylvania.

Dec. 6, 1849
- American abolitionist Harriet Tubman escapes from slavery.

Dec. 6 1897
- London becomes the world's First city to host licensed taxicabs.

Dec. 6, 1956
- Nelson Mandela and 156 others arrested for political activities in South Africa.

Dec 6, 1973
- Gerald Ford swom-in as first unelected Vice President, Succeeds Spiro T. Agnew.

Dec. 7, 1877
- Thomas. A. Edison demonstrates the gramophone.

Dec. 7, 1945
- Microwave oven patented

Dec. 7, 1975
- Indonesia invaded East Timor, leading to a 25-years occupation.

Dec. 7, 1982
- In Texas, Charles Brooks, Jr. becomes the first person to be executed by lethal injection in the United States.

Dec. 7, 2004
- Hamid Karzai was sworn in as Afghanistan's first Popularly elected president.

Dec. 8, 1941
- The United States entered World War II as Congress declared war against Japan, a day after the attack on Pearl Harbor.

Dec. 8, 1948
- UN approved the Recognition of South Korea.

Dec. 8, 1980
- John Lennon, a former member of the Beatles, the Rock group that transformed Popular music in the 1960s is shot and killed by an obsessed fan in New York City.

Dec 8, 1991
- The leaders of Russia, Belarus and Ukraine sign an agreement dissolving the soviet Union and establishing the commonwealth of Independent States.

Dec. 9, 1793
- The first daily newspaper in New York City was founded by Noah Webster. "The American Minerva" was Published for the first time this Day.

Dec. 9, 1872
- In Louisiana, P. B. S. Pinchback becomes the first Serving African-American governor of a U. S. state.

Dec. 9, 1905
- French Assembly National votes for separation of church and state

Dec. 9, 1908
- A child labor bill passes in the German Reichstag, Forbidding work for children under age 13.

DAYS OF HISTORY

Dec. 9, 1922
- Gabriel Narutowicz is announced the first president of Poland.

Dec. 9. 1931
- Spain becomes a republic

Dec. 9, 1948
- U. N. General Assembly unanimously approves Convention on Genocide

Dec. 9, 1949
- The United Nations takes trusteeship over Jerusalem.

Dec. 9, 1950
- President Harry Truman bans U. S. exports to Communist China.

Dec. 9, 1950
- Harry Gold gets 30 years imprisonment for passing atomic bomb secrets to the Soviet Union during World War II.

Dec. 9, 1953
- General Electric Announces all communist Employees will be fired

Dec. 9, 1961
- Tanganyika becomes Independent from Britain.

Dec. 9, 1961
- SS Col Adolf Eichmann Found guilty of war crimes in Israel

Dec. 9, 1963
- Zanzibar gains Independence from Britain

Dec. 9, 1967
- Nicolea Ceausescu becomes president (dictator) of Romania

Dec. 10, 1868
- The first traffic lights are installed, outside the Palace of Westminster in London. Resembling railway signals, they use semaphore arms and are illuminated at night by red and green gas lamps.

Dec. 10, 1901
- The first Nobel Prizes were awarded, in Stockholm, Sweden, in the fields of Physics, chemistry, Medicine, literature, and Peace.

Dec. 10, 1906
- U. S. President Theodore Roosevelt wins the Nobel Peace Prize, becoming the First American to win a Nobel Prize.

Dec. 11, 1917
- Lithuania declares its independence from Russia.

Dec. 11, 1937
- Second Italo- Abyssinian War: Italy leaves the League of Nations.

Dec. 11, 1958
- French Upper Volta Gains self-government from France, becomes the Republic of Upper Volta, and joins the French Community.

Dec. 11, 1962
- Arthur Lucas, convicted of murder, is the last person to be executed in Canada.

Dec. 11, 1964
- Che Guevara speaks at the United Nations General Assembly in New York City. An Unknown terrorist firs a mortar Shell at the building during the speech.

Dec. 11, 1972
- Apollo 17 becomes the sixth and last Apollo mission to land on the Moon.

Dec. 11, 1979
- Great Britain grants independence to Zimbabwe (Rhodesia)

Dec. 11, 1981
- U.N. Sec Council chose Javier Perez de Cuellar of Peru as 5th Secretary General.

DAYS OF HISTORY

Dec. 11, 1981
- It was Muhammad Ali's 61st and last fight. He lost to future champ Trevor Berbick

Dec. 11, 1994
- Russian troops invaded Chechnya in an Unsuccessful attempt to restore Moscow' power in the region.

Dec. 11, 2001
- The People's Republic of China joins the World Trade Organization.

Dec. 12, 1787
- Pennsylvania becomes the second state to ratify the United States Constitution Five days after Delaware became the first.

Dec. 12, 1822
Mexico was officially recognized as an independent nation by US.

Dec. 12, 1899
George F. Bryant of Boston Patented the wooden golf tee.

Dec. 12, 1925
Arthur Heinman opened the First motel, the "Motel Inn," in San Luis Obispo, Calif.

Dec 12, 1941
- Adolf Hitler announces extermination of the Jews at A meeting in the Reich Chancellery

Dec. 13, 1809
- Dr. Ephraim McDowell performed the first ovariotomy, removing atwenty-two pound tumor. The patient was Jane Todd Crawford and the operation Was performed without the aid of an anesthetic.

Dec. 13, 1918
- President Wilson arrived in France, becoming the first U. S. president to visit Europe while in office.

Dec. 13. 1960
- While Emperor Haile Selassie I of Ethiopia visits Brazil, his Imperial Bodyguard seizes the Deposed and his son, Crown Prince Asfa Wossen, Emperor.

Dec. 14, 1503
- French physician Nostradamus was born in St. Remy, Provence, France (as Michel de Notredame). He Wrote astrological predictions In rhymed quatrains, believed by many to foretell the future.

Dec. 14, 1751
- The Theresian Military Academy in Austria is Founded as the first Military Academy in the world.

Dec. 14, 1798
- David Wilkinson of Rhode Island patented the nut and Bolt machine, and the screw, 'too!

Dec 14, 1915
- Jack Johnson is first black World heavyweight boxing Champion.

Dec. 16, 1880
- Republic of South Africa forms.

Dec. 16, 1913
- Charlie Chaplin began his film career at Keystone for $150 a week.

Dec. 16, 1915
- Albert Einstein publishes the General Theory of Relativity.

Dec. 16, 1920
- One of the deadliest earthquakes in history hit the Gansu province in China. The 8.6 quake killed 200,000 people.

Dec. 16, 1949
- Chinese Communist leader Mao Tse-tung is Received at the Kremlin in Moscow.

DAYS OF HISTORY

Dec. 26, 1865
- James H. Nason received a patent for a coffee percolator.

Dec. 26, 1898
- Radium, the radioactive element, discovered by Pierre and Marie Curie

Dec. 26, 1972
- Uganda railroad from Mombassa to Lake Victoria is completed.

Dec. 26, 1964
- American Max Conrad Sets a new world non-stop-Flight record with his 7,878 Mile journey from Cape Town, south Africa, to St Petersburg, Florida.

Dec. 27, 1822
- Louis Pasteur (chemist, scientist: developed pasteurization process, rabies vaccination) was born on this day. (Died Sep 28, 1895)

Dec. 27, 1845
- Ether anesthetic is used for Childbirth for the first time by Dr. Crawford Williamson Long in Jefferson, Georgia.

Dec. 27, 1945
- The World Bank was created with the signing of an agreement by 28 nations.

Dec. 27, 1949
- The Netherlands transferred sovereignty to indonesia after more than 300 years of Dutch rule.

Dec. 28, 1612
- Galileo Galilei becomes the first astronomer to observe the planet Neptune, although he Mistakenly calatalogued it as a Fixed star.

Dec 28, 1694
- Queen Mary II of England died after five years of joint rule with her husband, King William III.

Dec. 28, 1795
- Construction of Yonge Street, formerly recognized as the longest street in the world, Begins in York, Upper Canada (present-day Toronto, Ontario).

Dec. 29, 1782
- First nautical almanac in U. S. published by Samuel Steams, Boston

Dec. 29, 1845
- In accordance with International Boundary delimitation, U. S. Aannexes the Mexican state of Texas, following the Manifest Destiny doctrine.

Dec. 29, 1891
- Thomas Edison of Milan, Ohio patented the radio

Dec. 29, 1908
- Patent granted for a 4-Wheel automobile brake, Clintonville

Dec. 29, 1911
- Mongolia gains independence from the Qing dynasty.

Dec. 29, 1922
- Revised Netherlands Law Proclaims suffrage.

Dec. 30, 1907
- Abraham Mills' commission declares Abner Doubleday invented baseball

Dec. 30, 1924
- Edwin Hubble announces the existence of other galaxies.

Dec. 30, 1965
- Ferdinand Marcos becomes President of the Philippines.

Dec. 30, 1999
- Former Beatle George Harrison was stabbed by an intruder at his home.

DAYS OF HISTORY

Dec. 30, 2006
- Deposed President of Iraq Saddam Hussein, convicted of the executions of 148 Iraqi Shiites, is executed by hanging.

Dec. 30, 2009
- The last roll of KodachromeFilm is developed by Dwayne's Photo.

Dec. 31, 1783
- Import of African slaves banned by all of the Northern States

Dec. 31, 1935
- Monopoly board game was patented by Charles B. Darrow, Pennsyvania, US.

Dec. 31, 1946
- President Truman officially proclaimed the end of hostilities in World War II.

Dec. 31, 1968
- First supersonic airliner flown (Russian TU-144)

Dec. 31, 1980
- Senegal president Leopold Senghor resigns

Dec. 31, 1981
- CNN Headline News debuts

Dec. 31, 1981
- Lt Jerry Rawlings becomes Head of Ghana, suspends Constitution.